Bessie Rayner Belloc

Historic Nuns

Bessie Rayner Belloc

Historic Nuns

ISBN/EAN: 9783742828552

Manufactured in Europe, USA, Canada, Australia, Japa

Cover: Foto ©ninafisch / pixelio.de

Manufactured and distributed by brebook publishing software (www.brebook.com)

Bessie Rayner Belloc

Historic Nuns

HISTORIC NUNS

By BESSIE R. BELLOC

Author of "In a Walled Garden," etc.

LONDON
DUCKWORTH & CO.
3 HENRIETTA STREET, W.C.
1898

A PREFATORY WORD

The sources of the following papers are these:—

1. For the Life of Mrs Aikenhead, the admirable and exhaustive Biography by Mrs Atkinson, "S. A."

2. For the Life of Mrs M'Aulay, an interesting book, presumably by a member of the Order of Mercy, published at New Orleans, and supplemented by the three volumes of Annals of the various foundations in different parts of the world.

3. For that of Madame Duchesne, the Life written in French by the Abbé Baunard, and translated by Lady Georgina Fullerton.

4. For that of Mrs Seton of Emmettsburg in Maryland, the Life written by the Rev. C. White, and containing her own diary and letters.

Furthermore, I would remark that an ever-growing body of literature exists in relation to the spiritual descendants of these four women and their work in England and America.

I have done my best to select and condense the materials as regards the Foundresses. The aftermath must be gathered by younger hands than mine.

Information in regard to the various books can be obtained at St Joseph's Library, South Street, Mayfair.

DEDICATED TO

SARAH (GAYNOR) ATKINSON

A THANK-OFFERING

CONTENTS

	PAGE
INTRODUCTION	1
I. MARY AIKENHEAD—	
1. CHARITY AND MERCY . . .	5
2. THE HEAT OF THE DAY . .	41
3. 1845. HAROLD'S CROSS . . .	63
II. CATHERINE M'AULAY . . .	75
III. MADAME DUCHESNE—	
1. SOLDIER AND MISSIONARY . .	128
2. WITH THE INDIANS AT LAST . .	168
3. THE LAST TEN YEARS . . .	178
IV. MOTHER SETON OF EMMETTSBURG . .	186
V. AN AMERICAN POSTSCRIPT . . .	215

HISTORIC NUNS

INTRODUCTION

In attempting to present historical pictures verbally, the first question to be resolved is—to what extent transcripts of original material should be faithfully used in order to impress great personalities on the minds of those who either do desire, or can be induced to desire, to know something about them, and to fathom the springs of their extraordinary achievements. The original biography is always necessarily there, made either by someone who knew the subject (as in de Joinville's exquisite account of St Louis, or Boswell's inimitable Life of Johnson), or who possessed, in addition, a special access to private letters and contemporaneous memoranda; such full knowledge as resulted in one of the most remarkable biographies of modern times,—that of Mrs Aikenhead, by S. A., a book specially referred to by Mr Lecky, and calculated to cause despair in the mind of anyone, however well versed in literary methods, who presumes to touch the same theme. For why should anyone meddle with that which has already been perfectly done? And I would not attempt it did I not know that humbler pens may find their use in helping to diffuse a knowledge of work possessing massive power and authority,—that a torch may reflect light on Michael Angelo's Moses.

In regard to the second Foundress with whose life and labours I propose to deal, readers can find more than one account of her experiences and labours, lovingly compiled, rather than artistically condensed, by those who had personally known her, and regarded her memory with fond reverence. A mass of material exists concerning Mrs Catherine M'Aulay, and the Life which was immediately available to me was published in America. It is full of interest and sap, but every page is written entirely from the inside, and takes for granted the highest supernatural motives, unveiling with more or less frankness the deepest religious emotions of the various actors on the scene, showing them as they really were in their thoughts and at their prayers. Such original material strikes at the heart of the reader by the inevitable impact of the saint. And lives transfused by the radiance of faith create their own public. The incidents and the anecdotes take root, they are repeated by the old to the young, and re-copied for the spiritual descendant. St Augustine makes a confession, St Francis discourses to the birds and the fishes: one writes a letter of advice, another composes a prayer, a third launches a hymn. These are struck off at white-heat, and are a legacy to all the world. To me they seem the highest triumph of the written word. The imagination of man cannot create anything so vivid as the unpremeditated revelation of man himself.

INTRODUCTION

Nevertheless, of the labours of those who have greatly blessed mankind, and who have moved masses of fellow-beings to positive, practical action, it is natural to desire a connected picture, or an abridged and compacted story, if only to point the way to more real, because original, sources of information. We may record the strategy of a great general, apart from the intimate details of the hero's private existence. And, moreover, the Founders, the builders up of great works, they who set their walls about the city and their towers upon the hills, pass away; and the print of their own footsteps over the vast length of the Empire are visible signs of men and women, not only beloved by their own people, but architects in stone and wood, and truly also of temples not made with hands. Their followers can be counted by thousands, and many among these also became great educators, great protectors of youth, great tenders of the sick and the dying. Some among them made long voyages, plunged into new colonies, lived strenuous lives, and, whether at home or abroad, died when necessary as fearlessly as any soldiers of the thin red line. By times their experiences read like a child's tale of adventure, and nearly all are full of the romance of heroism, and stand high above the flat average of human days. And the transcriber picks and chooses, and wonders what to put in and what to omit, haunted by a sense of numbers, like that great Seer of Patmos, who heard the voice from heaven as the voice of many waters, and enumerates the great multitude who had the Father's name written on their foreheads, and were redeemed from the earth.

It would be all too easy to wrap a veil of poetic mist round any story which begins in Ireland. She is, to those who love her, a land of faith and romance, of ardent emotion, of the yearning of the exile, of the graves of the dearest, of song human and divine. But, just because of this glamour, some very salient points of her history are absolutely ignored, although absolutely real; a veil has dropped between them and contemporary history. Good people are apt to grieve for Ireland, but they look at her with a singularly uncomprehending gaze, with sympathetic eyes, in which pity holds too large a place. Let us pity her no more, but look steadily at the splendid achievements by which she will best be known. Her feet may have been among the briars, but she, at least, has not missed the way. Within the short space of one hundred years the Irish people have created two great instruments of help, which, for energy and efficiency, have been quite unrivalled in the history of our English-speaking race. We struggle with our social inequalities, we lament the state of our poor, we do a great deal—we do, on the whole, what we can; we hammer at legislation, we chisel at Charity Organisation. It is not money which fails; our trouble is that we are consumed by doubts of what best to do. The answer has come to us across the sea—a gentle answer, devoid of controversy, spoken by the voices of women. It comes from those who can say they "believe and hope."

MARY AIKENHEAD

Chapter I

CHARITY AND MERCY

In writing of the two Institutions which have deeply stamped themselves and their methods of work upon the Empire and on the United States of America, priority must be assigned to that of the Irish Sisters of Charity as the first in the order of time. It is less known in England, having been especially created for the needs of the Irish people at home and in America, whither it has followed them; but it came into being some twenty years earlier than the Order of Mercy, and its powers of expansion would have been equal had its purpose been identical.

Mary Aikenhead and Catherine M'Aulay were born in the same year, 1787, but the former was earlier called to a definite religious vocation. There was also a marked difference in the methods by which the orders were gradually formed. That of Charity was planned for home needs by an eminent priest, who selected Mary Aikenhead as the fittest instrument of his purpose, before she had attained her thirtieth year.

The Rev. Daniel Murray, born in 1768, who lived to be eighty-five, and died Archbishop of Dublin, leaving a great name behind him, was not quite forty, and still a curate, when he first met Miss

Aikenhead in her native city of Cork. He had been educated partly in Dublin and partly in Salamanca, from which Spanish college he had returned at the age of twenty-two, after a residence of six years. Ordained in 1790, he served as curate in his native town of Arklow, in Wicklow, for some years; his mother still lived in the old home, and was happy in the ministrations of her son. But in the fatal year of 1798 Arklow was "the scene of a terrible affray; the old parish priest was murdered in his bed, and his curate escaped by a sort of miracle, for he was fired at as he crossed the river at Shelton Abbey. His only safety was in flight; and so, taking horse, he rode to Dublin by a route full of difficulties and danger." In the city he lived for many years as curate, firstly in the parish of St Andrew and afterwards in that of St Mary, of which latter charge it is said that he laboured "in the midst of a multitudinous flock, destitute of nearly all the common resources of a Catholic community. It was enough to make his heart sink within him to witness the misery accumulated in the crowded back streets and lanes of the metropolitan parish, and to look around in vain for any adequate means of relieving their temporal distress or ministering to their grievous spiritual needs." Such are the words in which S. A. emphasises the anxieties which were to result in the foundation of the Institute of the Sisters of Charity, when, in later years, the zealous curate became coadjutor in the See of Dublin, and finally Archbishop of Dublin, on the death of the aged Dr Troy.

Meantime, the woman who was to give such efficient help to Dr Murray was growing from childhood into youth, and from youth into ardent, intelligent young womanhood, under mingled influences, which are admirably described by her biographer. Mary Aikenhead was the daughter of a Protestant physician of Scottish descent. Her grandfather, David Aikenhead, held a commission in the 26th Cameronian Regiment, but relinquished the military profession, and married a Limerick lady, settling permanently in Ireland. The wife was daughter to Mr Rice Wight, of the same family as that now represented by Lord Monteagle, and their son was thus "born in the Hanoverian ranks." David Aikenhead the younger, however, fell in love with a Catholic girl, Mary Stacpole, and married her with the consent of her parents, guaranteeing the free exercise of her religion, but stipulating that all the children of the marriage should be brought up as Protestants. Nevertheless, so closely connected were the different sections of the Irish population in the last century that the eldest little daughter was put out to nurse in a humble family devoted to the ancient faith, and remained with them until she was six years old. In more than one instance, as we turn over the records of Ireland before the Union, we find the Protestants so completely dominant in their own imagination as to be oblivious of influences destined to slowly but surely tell upon their children. Apparently they did not realise that educated people could really, seriously, adopt the religion of the peasant and the foster-mother. As soon might the little white baby of one of the Southern United States change its colour when confided to the tender care of a black mammy or auntie, as little Hanoverian babies lisp the Hail Mary, or touch their own little brows with the Sign of the Cross! Be that as it may, the little girl was thus early habituated to regard the faith of the people with tenderness, and her father, originally a strong Protestant, seems gradually to have come under the same influences. He retired from his profession with a competence in 1798, and "found himself free to form another plan of life from that which he had followed with credit and success." But his time was indeed shortened. Dr Aikenhead's health declined, and before the last days of 1801 he was past recovery. Then it was that his wife's extreme distress moved him to seriously examine the claims of her religion; he sent for a priest, and applied his mind to the subject. Finally, the Scotch doctor made his profession of faith, and on the 28th of December breathed his last amidst the tears and prayers of his family. Six months later, in June 1802, his young daughter of fifteen followed her father into the Catholic Church, and thus it was that the Irish Sisters of Charity gained their foundress.

Two younger girls were sent to the Ursuline Convent of Cork, to be educated with their cousins, the Hennesseys, nieces of Mrs Aikenhead, and the family continued to dwell in that city, in comfortable circumstances, and in the enjoyment of a lively and intellectual society. Ireland, a hundred years ago, was much more closely connected with France than she now is. Nearly all the Catholic heads of families in Mary Aikenhead's youth had been educated on the Continent, and French was taught to their children by thoroughly competent professors. Both the descendants of Huguenot soldiers, and the Catholic priests trained in foreign colleges, kept up the tradition that it was necessary to "speak French like a native." The closing of the Continent by the Napoleonic wars had not had time to change the habit of many generations. At the Peace of Amiens, in 1802, occurred a general rush across the Channel of those who could afford to travel, and a not inconsiderable number became *détenus* when the Emperor suddenly re-closed the gates. The same thing occurred twelve years later, during the Hundred Days, when fathers even hurried their young daughters across to the long barred Paris, that they might see the wonderful trophies from every country in Europe accumulated in the Louvre. Mrs Siddons was one of those who thus went over, and was seen by a young English girl standing in front of the Apollo Belvidere; and heard observing sonorously, "So stands the statue which enchants the world."

Doubtless, Cork and Dublin furnished their contingent of eager travellers. S. A. tell us that not only the heads of families but many of the younger men had actually got more or less schooling on the Continent before the Revolution broke out. "Many of the merchants having relatives on the Continent, had seen foreign life in their company other than student-wise, and still kept up friendly intercourse with them. Not a few of humbler standing had also their foreign connections, and though living in poor circumstances received letters and presents from relatives in high station abroad. Oftentimes the souvenirs sent home were a touching evidence of the exile's undying recollection of the old land and faithful love of kindred; yet withal provoked a smile, so ludicrously out of character with the condition of the recipients were the exquisite pieces of art workmanship, and the articles of court costume transmitted to the humble inheritors of once renowned names." And on another page we find that "although the Protestant minority with their jealously guarded privileges, and the Catholic majority with their vexatious disabilities, continued to form two distinct classes, which only now and then entered into really cordial relations, society in Cork was, nevertheless, pervaded with a general tone, distinguishing it favourably from that of other places. As a whole, the citizens were a highly intelligent, humorous race, who understood the art of enjoying life as well as the art of enriching themselves by commercial enterprise." They were a polite as well as a witty people, they cultivated music in earnest, "following, though at a humble distance, the example set them in his day by Bishop Berkeley, who had an eminent Italian master domesticated in his palace at Cloyne, and used to call up his children at cock-crow to practise on different instruments, and go through their singing lessons in the golden dawn." They were also very fond of flowers, and "the merchant residences, situated on the slope of wooded hills, washed by the sparkling river, and looking out on a landscape of rare sylvan beauty, were rendered still more picturesque by their setting of tasteful shrubberies and brilliant parterres, which expanded and glowed under the gently stimulating influence of an atmosphere permeated with heat, and charged with moisture." They were also much devoted to theatrical amusements, and the great London actors, Garrick, the Kembles, and Mrs Siddons, were far from indifferent to their verdicts; while the Cork circuit boasted first of Curran, and then of O'Connell, and the "bar all through was brilliant in the extreme." I quote without remorse from S. A.'s charming pages, happy if they do but lead the reader to the book.

In this bright society Mary Aikenhead shone among the other girls by unusual intelligence and a winning exterior. "No young lady was more in request as a partner; she was a first-rate dancer, light of step, and easy of carriage in the country dance, but excelling in the minuet." She was, however, handsome rather than pretty, "with expressive changeful eyes, which some said were grey, and others believed to be bright hazel, and others pronounced the very next thing to jet black. But neither the amusements natural to a girl in her 'teens, nor the large share which she early took in the management of the house property, in which Dr Aikenhead had largely invested his money, absorbed the mind and heart of young Mary Aikenhead. A deep strain of piety was hidden under her cheerful capable exterior. At whatever hour she returned from a party she was observed to be punctual at the ten o'clock mass next morning, and "some who had the opportunity of observing her still more closely, confidentially informed their gossips that she used to burn down a whole mould candle while saying her prayers after she had been out at a dance." And this piety took a most practical shape; she was indefatigable among the poor of her native town, from whom the doctor's daughter never felt herself to be apart. From early childhood she cherished the ideal of a life devoted to their service, in connection with some form of the religious life.

But there was no order, nor had there ever been an order, in Ireland whose rule included the relief of the poor in their own homes, or the reception of the sick in hospitals. Nuns of any kind were very rare, and what there were were strictly enclosed. Any personage similar to a French Sister of Charity seen in the open street had been hitherto impossible. The Ursuline and Presentation nuns taught multitudes of children in the beginning of this Century, but within their own walls. As Mary Aikenhead neared her twentieth year she seemed strongly attracted to the Presentation Order, and but for a promise made to a close friend, who had been her associate in charitable work, she would probably have cast in her lot with them. Miss Cecilia Lynch was preparing to enter an enclosed convent near Dublin, and she begged Mary Aikenhead to come to no decision until this convent had been visited. But

Cork was then a long way from Dublin, and Mary Aikenhead had no friends in the metropolis. So probable did it seem that she would be hidden in a life of useful obscurity. But God had another purpose for her. When Mary was twenty years old a young lady, Miss Cecilia Ball, was professed at the Ursuline Convent in Cork, and to the ceremony came her two sisters, Miss Fanny Ball and Mrs John O'Brien. The latter lady, a marked figure in the best Dublin society, not much older than Mary herself, was attracted by the interesting girl, and invited her to Dublin and thus changed the whole current of a life. Thenceforward, for some few years, Mary Aikenhead was associated by occasional visits with a wealthy and prosperous circle in the metropolis. "Mrs O'Brien's father, Mr Ball, had in pre-union times amassed a considerable fortune in the silk trade, which, introduced into Dublin by the Huguenot refugees and fostered by their industry, had become a flourishing branch of manufacture." The Balls were an important family in other ways, and Mrs O'Brien's only brother was ultimately the second Catholic raised to the judicial bench after the emancipation. The O'Briens were also in good circumstances, and remarkable for "their charity to the poor and liberality to the clergy and the few institutions it had been possible to establish in the difficult times not yet passed away." It was, therefore, a busy working world of benevolence into which the young visitor from Cork found herself initiated. It was in 1808 that the first visit took place, and in 1809 that it was repeated; but in the interval a great change in Mary Aikenhead's life had taken place. Her good, pious mother was suddenly taken ill, and died in three days, leaving her eldest child in sole charge of the household and affairs. The two young sisters were placed as boarders in the Ursuline Convent, and Miss Aikenhead, though for the moment personally free, could not contemplate any step which would really break up the home.

We turn now to Dr Murray, who in 1809 was consecrated Coadjutor Bishop of Dublin, and entertained a fixed intention of founding a congregation of active unenclosed nuns. Such were then, as I have said, quite unknown in Ireland, but the race of priests educated in France were familiar with the French Sisters of St Vincent de Paul. One day, during Mary's visit of 1809 to Mrs O'Brien, the two friends went to the convent of Poor Clares at Harold's Cross, where dwelt in religious seclusion the old Cork friend, Cecilia Lynch, who had been accustomed to visit the poor with Miss Aikenhead in former days. The nun told her friend that Dr Murray wished to found an active congregation and had proposed to her to "remain disengaged" till he could make his arrangements, "but," added the nun, "not feeling up to the responsibility of a new order, I preferred remaining where I am." "O Cecilia," exclaimed Mary Aikenhead, with uncommon earnestness, "why did you not wait?" Mrs O'Brien, who was present, repeated this speech to Dr Murray, who did not forget it. The next link in the chain of circumstances was a visit paid by the Bishop of Cork to Dublin; *he* knew Mary Aikenhead well at home, and on one occasion when she was in the company of the two prelates, the young girl turned to her own bishop exclaiming, "Oh! my lord, when will you bring Sisters of Charity to Cork?" So that both the good men foresaw in her a future helper, and Mary, when sounded on the subject, replied that "if an efficient superior and two or three members undertook the work, she should certainly think that in joining them she was doing what God required of her." In the meantime she could not give up her home, and Dr Murray assured her that until her sisters were older she was the "only parent" they had to look to. Only, if one were settled so as to be a protector to the other, she might then very wisely think of devoting herself to the life of an active religious. He gave her no hint whatever that his plans could in any way be dependent on her future co-operation.

The Bishop of Cork did not long survive this visit to Dublin, and his end was a notable one. He had not quite reached his fiftieth year when he "fell a victim to one of the terrible fevers which constantly swept like a plague over the towns and rural districts of Ireland. Passing through a street in which the fever was raging, he was asked to enter a house to see a dying man. A neighbour tried to dissuade him from risking his own valuable life, but the Bishop answered, 'I will go and save that soul!' He did all that could be done for the dying man, took the contagion, and after ten days' illness himself died on the 19th June 1810."

While Dr Murray pondered his future plans, Mary Aikenhead helped her friend Mrs O'Brien to start a refuge for girls of good character in the city of Dublin, both the friends understanding that it was to be given over to Dr Murray's new order when it got under weigh. But it was not an easy matter to introduce into Ireland any institution resembling that of St Vincent de Paul in France. No direct communication with Paris existed during those years of the Napoleonic wars, and therefore, of course, no direct affiliation to the Order of St Vincent was possible. But as soon as the Bishop judged it right and possible for Mary to absent herself from her younger sisters, he seems to have said to her that his great dependence was actually upon her co-operation, causing her thereby "unspeakable amazement." She yielded to his wish, but besought Dr Murray that she might be regularly trained in an institute where "the duties resembled, in some degree, those proposed to be carried out in the new foundation." This was more than difficult to find. Neither in England nor in Ireland were there, at that time, any nuns resembling those various Sisters with whom, under one name or another, we are now so very familiar, and the only available step forward proved to be that of entering into communication with the famous old House at York, popularly called the "Bar Convent," from its being situated close to Micklegate Bar. This was chiefly known as a school for young ladies, but the nuns were not enclosed, and naturally went out to visit the sick. The House dated back from 1685, and had managed to hold on through the flight of James II., through the reigns of William and Mary, and Queen Anne, and even those of the Georges. The ladies were forced to wear a secular "matronly dress," and continued to wear it for one hundred and twenty years. The story of the Bar Convent bristles thick with English names—Bedingfield, Gascoigne, Thring, and Babthorpe, among others. It was Mrs Francis Bedingfield, daughter of a Suffolk gentleman, and formerly superioress of a number of English ladies settled in Germany, who first came back to her native land entrusted with the perilous task of founding a convent in England, in 1669. She had much difficulty and trouble, in spite of the help and sympathy of the two Catholic Queens, and, after a long struggle, the Sisterhood were again nearly uprooted in the Jacobite insurrection of 1745, receiving peremptory orders to quit the house immediately, under threats of the execution of the penal laws. But they managed to lie low, and on the cessation of the political agitation caused by the rising, they seem to have remained unmolested. "Encouraged by the hospitable reception accorded to the several religious communities which took refuge in England on the outbreak of the French Revolution, the sixth superioress of the York Convent, Reverend Mother Ronby, and her nuns ventured to resume the religious habit, and about twenty years later they resumed religious names." This long passage of time brings us to the year 1814, when Mary Aikenhead and an Irish lady named Miss Alicia Walsh had been for two years inmates of the Bar Convent. The particulars quoted above are from Mr John Nicholas Murphy's most interesting book, "Terra Incognita."

Miss Walsh was fourteen years older than her young friend, who was five-and-twenty when the pair started for York in 1812. Not much is known of how the former came to interest herself so deeply in Dr Murray's project. She became the much-beloved Mother Catherine, associated with all the early struggles of the Institute, and to her we shall recur.

In 1814, just as the two Irish Sisters expected to return home, came the episode of the Hundred Days, and the consequent re-opening of the Continent, and Dr Murray found himself summoned to Rome in company with the English Bishop, Dr Milner, and in passing through France he conferred with the Superior-General of the French Sisters of Charity, and a question of possible affiliation seems to have arisen, but it came to nothing; acceptance would have involved the bringing over of three French Sisters to form the establishment, and the entire adoption of the ancient rule of St Vincent de Paul, which was judged difficult and unsuitable for the state of Ireland at that time. The magnificent order of "the White Cornettes" is essentially French in conception, and in the details of its rule. It is also, however, especially available in London, where it was implanted fifty years later than the time of which we are now speaking, and where there is so large a foreign population. Ireland had other needs, and "the idea of making a foundation according to the *projet d'accord* with the Sisters of St Vincent de Paul was entirely abandoned." S. A.'s account of the successive consultations and negotiations on this matter is extremely interesting, and well worth consulting as an example of the preliminary care and thought exercised by the authorities of the Church in regard to new foundations.

Thus it came to pass that the two Irish ladies spent a third year at York. They "never assumed the dress of the Institute but wore the plain black gown, the cap and veil of the postulant. They took, however, with permission, the religious names which they bore till death." Mrs Aikenhead that of Mary Augustine, and Mrs Walsh that of Mary Catherine, after the Saint of Sienna, "to whom she had a special devotion, and whose charity for the sick and the afflicted, for poor prisoners and sinners led astray, she always strove to imitate."

It was in the month of August 1815, before tears were dried for the dead of the field of Waterloo, that Dr Murray found himself at last able to go to England and fetch Mrs Aikenhead and Mrs Walsh home. He had made all his fatherly preparations for their reception in Dublin, had got a house for them in William Street on the north side of the city, had enlarged it, and had built a pretty little chapel, for which the money was largely provided by Miss Denis, a friend and fellow-worker of the indefatigable Mrs O'Brien. His journey was a long undertaking then; but the Bishop was only just past middle age, and in the prime of experience and resolution. We must conceive of him as starting on a sailing packet on the 13th of August and taking five days to get to York on the other side of England. Glad must his countrywomen have been to see him! He lost, however, no time, for that very same day he started homewards with his two charges, and on the 22nd they "sailed into the Bay of Dublin with a favourable wind and stepped on shore exulting." Yet no sooner had they passed twenty-four hours in their new home than a most unwelcome thing occurred. Dr Murray found himself again obliged to start without delay for Rome, to conduct some delicate negotiations for the Irish bishops, who were alarmed at the prospect of a veto being granted to the King, or rather to the Prince Regent, then acting for his insane father.

The Bishop, with "characteristic energy and decision," arranged for his two postulants to be professed before his departure. On the 1st of September they made their vows for one year. Mary Aikenhead, then twenty-eight years old, he nominated Superior-General; Mrs Walsh, Mistress of Novices; and two days later he received the first postulant of the infant community, Miss Catherine Lynch of Drogheda. On the next day he authorised exactly that which St Teresa invariably first besought when starting her foundations (St Teresa who is warmly but somewhat vaguely admired in England). Benediction of the Blessed

Sacrament was given in the convent chapel, and the tabernacle became the centre of all its life and work.

The endless laborious detail of gradually and canonically building up the order of the Irish Sisters of Charity need not be further described. It has been admirably unravelled from the original documents by S. A., and is in its way very interesting reading, possessing the same sort of interest which for many minds is attached to the building up of a constitutional or economic system. It may be shortly summed up that the initiative was entirely due to one man, a middle-aged Irish bishop, and that he selected as helper and instrument the daughter of a physician, a bright girl of whom nothing could at first be predicted but that she was ardently devoted to the poor; that Dr Murray waited for several years until Miss Aikenhead was righteously free from domestic ties, and then sent her and an older companion to be trained in a very old English convent, where the nuns had from generation to generation been accustomed to visit the poor in their own homes. And the reason of his choice of a training home was that no such thing had ever been seen or had been in any way possible in Ireland, owing to the greater pressure of the penal laws.

It must also be again remarked that although in the last century the Irish priesthood were trained on the Continent, in France and in Spain, and that in France they were familiar with the Sisters of St Vincent de Paul, who went about freely, yet during those years of planning and preparation France was entirely closed both to the English and the Irish by the war with Napoleon. It was still so closed in 1812, when at the age of five-and-twenty Mary Aikenhead went to York, but we then had amongst us a great population of *emigrés* who had familiarised the English people with their ideas and their worship, and traces of this emigration are to be seen in our literature of the date. Miss Edgeworth wrote a charming story about a nun and her school children in the midst of the Revolution, opening with a pretty scene of the roasting of chestnuts in a little Dutch oven; Miss Edgeworth knew France very well and described vividly what she had seen. This was, I think, the very first time that anybody had made a good brave heroine out of a nun. Previous to that the romancers had immured them in dungeons, walled them up alive, carried them off on wild horses, drowned them in tears, or left them weltering in their blood. We may also recall a charming picture by Miss Mitford of the old French Abbé who taught her French. A true and delicate image, totally unlike Cardinal Richelieu, or the Abbé Dubois, or a Spanish Inquisitor, or the learned and courtly Erasmus. Here we have a real French priest giving French lessons in Hans Place, Chelsea, to a number of little English girls, one of whom was a true artist in portraiture, and has preserved his memory well.

In Dr Murray and Mary Aikenhead we contemplate people of the generation immediately preceding our own, known to innumerable people now living.

MRS AIKENHEAD

For instance, Dr Murray ordained the priest of the parish in which these lines are penned (dying himself at eighty-five), and Mary Aikenhead's own spiritual daughters are still many of them alive, immersed in work *this* week, *last* week, and the week before that!

Returning to our dates, we must consider the original little community as fairly started in 1815, but it was two more years before they changed their simple black dress and muslin cap for the costume now dear and familiar to those who love them. It is of plain black stuff, with an ample veil. The sleeves are wide, the guimpe is black, and no white is seen except in the folds of linen about the face and throat. "One thing alone is brilliant—the solid, broad, brass cross, bearing the image of the crucified Saviour on one side, which is suspended on the breast and shines in sunlight or lamplight like a gem in a dusky setting. Suspended from the girdle are the rosary beads and the steel chains, to which are attached scissors, keys, and other requisites for the sick-room or the workroom." And these first years were spent in William Street, where the nuns, few in number and limited in means, found their work constantly increasing. In 1818 they lost two very useful members of the congregation by death; one of them caught a fever in the third month after her profession, and "this first death, so like a sacrificial rite of solemn significance, made a profound impression on the little community. Mrs Aikenhead, when alluding to the circumstance thirty-three years later, said that the impression made on her was so awful, deep, and lasting that she never attempted to describe what she felt." For a month previous to the death Mrs Aikenhead sat up with the patient every night, allowing herself very little rest in the daytime. The strain was terribly severe, and her road practically untrodden. "In Ireland precedent could not be cited in any case that came before her for consideration. Here, religious had never hitherto been brought into daily, almost hourly, communication with the world." She herself was now thirty-one years old, and singularly prepossessing in the dignity of her religious garb. "A noble looking woman." "When silent she often had a preoccupied, almost a severe look, but when she spoke it seemed as if the countenance conveyed more than the words, and registered with greater fidelity any change of feeling. Whether she spoke or whether she was silent the beautiful well-set eyes dominated the face."

It was in 1819, four years after the formal commencement of Mrs Aikenhead's work, that a very important move was made. For several years a group of Dublin ladies, with the clever, bright, and excellent Mrs O'Brien at their head, had been associated in the care of a refuge for respectable working girls, orphans, and others. In 1814, this refuge had been moved to a site in Stanhope Street, a place so dear and familiar to the writer of these lines that a short description of it may not be amiss. It is still almost out of Dublin, on the north side, and the old house, standing in a very large garden, near the top of a steep hill, must at one time have commanded a great view across the Liffey to "Patrick's" and Christchurch. But all the slope beneath it is chiefly built up with what are now very poor streets; and a little above the gate is the large pile of Richmond Jail. The house has a low square parlour, and a charming staircase leading to old rooms, but beside it rises the pile of new buildings, which the Sisters have made notable all over the world, and a church stands in the great garden, and beyond the garden are now the new schools. All these must disappear from the mental picture of the place in 1814. But the beds of mignonette and the gay old flowers running up under the old-fashioned windows were sweet and blooming then as they are to-day. For five years Mrs O'Brien and her friends collected their girls here, taught them, trained them, and started them in life as best they could, and at last pressed the Sisters in William Street to make a foundation on the spot, and take charge of the institution. To build a chapel and cells for the nuns required money; a good friend (Miss Denis again) gave nearly a thousand pounds to Dr Murray for the purpose. The place was in sufficient readiness in January 1819, and Dr Murray arranged for the taking over of the refuge by the Sisters. On the evening of the 29th Mrs Aikenhead and Sister Mary Joseph O'Reilly were conveyed thither by Mrs O'Brien. It was a cold dreary evening; everything had been upset by the building operations, and the impression made on the new inmates was anything but cheerful. However, with the assistance of three young women who were in the House of Refuge as aids, order was so far established that on the 2nd of February, the Feast of the Purification, Dr Murray celebrated the first mass in the new chapel and blessed the house. These three young women afterwards joined the order as domestic Sisters.

Such was the beginning of the convent at Stanhope Street, and from 1819 to 1826 Mrs Aikenhead lived there, leaving the house in North William Street, and all its works, in the "very efficient hands" of Mother Catherine. At Stanhope Street, Mrs Aikenhead "devoted herself mainly to the task of training the younger members of the now steadily-increasing congregation, without, however, neglecting the visitation and relief of the poor in their homes, or any of the other exterior duties of a Sister of Charity." And for more than eighty years, seventy-eight of which have passed under the rule of the order, these works of mercy have here been carried on with unceasing fidelity. "Ohne Hast, ohne Rast."

And, moreover, as these details are in process of being extracted from S. A.'s book on a Sunday morning, this very afternoon will see the young women employed in Dublin houses of business flocking up to a service in the convent church, and gathering in a long procession which files through the old garden to the sound of hymns and prayers.

These two convents, which for some years contained all the Sisters of Charity, gradually increased their numbers, and in the first year of the new installation two of the nuns in the older foundation began to visit one of the Dublin hospitals, accompanied by their usual lay-helper, who seems to have been almost ubiquitous in well-doing; while from Stanhope Street Mrs Aikenhead herself went with a companion to open Sunday classes at the parochial schools in Abbey Street.

In 1821 a very painful duty was imposed upon them, when the Governor of Kilmainham Gaol requested Dr Murray to send the nuns to visit two young women who, having been convicted of murder, were in prison under sentence of death. It may be well conceived that such a task was not delegated by the unsparing, devoted woman whose life we follow. Mary Aikenhead, then four-and-thirty years old, went herself, taking with her that older nun, Mother Catherine, who had been her first companion. On this first visit they were accompanied by a priest and Mrs O'Brien, afterwards they went alone. One of the unhappy young women had lived near the convent in North William Street, and was known to the nuns. The parish priest and his curate, the Rev. William Yore, also made frequent and effectual visits, and on the morning of the execution Mary Aikenhead and Mother Catherine "conducted the poor women to the chapel, where the doomed creatures and their consoling visitors remained from nine o'clock till two, the hour appointed for the execution. Then the women were led out by the governor, the nuns remained in the chapel, and did not leave it till two hours after the execution." Mr

Yore went to the gallows, on the outer wall of the prison, in full view of an enormous crowd, and "remained with them till the last moment, sending his prayers with theirs up to the throne of mercy." He never could henceforth forget the "horrifying shock." What a ghastly story, and what a power of grace and will to enable two such women as Mary Aikenhead and her friend to endure the protracted agonies of such a day, and survive it!

Our next picture of the reverend Mother is of a cheerful and consolatory nature. In 1826 she revisited her beloved native city of Cork, the motive being an urgent, and indeed repeated, application for a convent of the Sisters of Charity on the part of the Bishop. The matter lay in the hands of Dr Murray, and as soon as he judged the Dublin houses sufficiently established to bear the loss of several of their members, it was arranged that the Bishop of Cork should come to Dublin for the purpose of accompanying to that city the foundress herself and another Sister (Mrs Teeling), who were to precede the regular colony, and prepare for their reception. "On the 25th of September Mary Aikenhead, in the still glow of an autumn evening, saw again, as the carriage drove into the city, all the familiar features of her birthplace—the quays, the bridges, the glancing river, Shandon steeple upon the heights. She recognised the bright, kindly faces, and heard, not without emotion, the soft, southern Corkonian brogue." Her father's old servant, in whose cottage she had been put to nurse, was "determined to have the first word with Miss Mary," and he went to the Bishop's house and stood in the hall ready to receive her; and S. A. tells us with peculiar tenderness how Miss Mary, at sight of him, cried out, "O Daddy John," and threw her arms round the neck of her dear old foster-father and kissed him, while "the Bishop's servant, who stood by with his best manners on, and wholly unprepared for this scene, lifted up his hands in amazement to see the greeting which took place between Daddy John and the great Mother Abbess from Dublin."

She had to wait six weeks before things were in sufficient readiness to allow of her sending for more sisters from Dublin. The house intended for their habitation stood close to the cathedral and presbytery, and was surrounded by lanes and the crowded dwellings of the poor. It was old, shabby, and of no particular style of architecture; it was also "high, narrow, crooked, with ladder-like stairs, a questionable roof, and walls which all the whitewash in the world could not coax into looking secure." It lacked a garden, and even a good yard. People looked at it disdainfully as they passed by. What the reverend Mother felt at the first sight of it is not told, but she "was never the first to see a lion in the way." In those days of small beginnings, it was an excellent thing to get a house at all, and the Sisters, among themselves, gave it the affectionate name of Cork Castle! The workmen were turned in, and Mrs Aikenhead and Mrs Teeling spent their leisure in going to see old friends among the poor, when they could do so without having to walk through the streets, "where the sight of a nun would have caused no small astonishment." Sometimes, however, they were taken farther afield in some kind friend's carriage. One day, passing along Pope's Quay, the reverend Mother said to her companion, pointing to one of the houses: "Do you know how I went to my last party in that house? In a boat, my dear!"

Of course she went to see her foster-mother, Mary Rorke, the wife of Daddy John, and fifty years afterwards the visit was related in full by a granddaughter, a little child at the time, who had been badly burned, and was being nursed at her grandmother's, "when suddenly one day she saw a carriage drive into the lane and stop at the door, and saw a lovely nun get out accompanied by another nun and a priest, and the first nun went over to the granny and kissed her, and there was great joy: for it was Miss Mary come from Dublin. And there was another old woman in the room at the time, and the granny said: 'Don't you remember Mary Lyons, your own kitchen-maid?' and Miss Mary put out her hand to her; but the old woman was not for shaking hands, because she was after dressing the wounds, but Miss Mary insisted. The child never afterwards forgot that scene, nor the beautiful looking woman whom the granny called Miss Mary."

At the end of the six weeks, the four nuns from Dublin "told off," like soldiers, for duty in Cork, were able to start. They were two days on the road, and were carefully escorted by a priest, Father Charles Aylmer. Those were days when ladies were not supposed to go travelling about by the stage coach without due protection. The Bishop sent vehicles to meet them at the coach office and bring them to his own house to dinner, where the clergyman of the parish had been invited to meet them. In the evening the six nuns took possession of the new convent.

The next day they were taken by the Bishop to visit the Ursulines, who had then, as now, a large school for young ladies, and who had been dear friends of Mary Aikenhead's in her youth. Here they found a young Sister, whose name in the world had been Eliza Anster, and who had been partly educated in France, at the convent of Les Dames Anglaises in Paris, where George Sand was also a pupil. In the memoirs of the latter is a well-known, but most eloquent and interesting description of the English girl who afterwards became Sister Augustine at Cork. Shortly before her death Madame Sand wrote a loving letter to her old friend, Mrs Anster. The long note in which S. A. speaks of the renewed correspondence is well worth quoting, but I refer readers to the book itself, and also to the fine description of the Parisian convent and its Sisterhood, in the "Histoire de ma Vie."

A fortnight after the arrival of the Dublin contingent, "Cork Castle" was in full work. The day of the actual foundation of the House is noted as the 13th of November, the Feast of St Stanislaus. Their chapel was well fitted up by zealous friends, and when *that* is in order, all nuns consider themselves well started. But Cork Castle was doubtless also supplied with suitable domestic necessaries by those who loved the inmates, and well it was, for they were shortly to endure a terrible ordeal.

On the 19th of that same month of inauguration the Sisters began visiting the poor. As it was the first time nuns had ever been seen in the streets, they were at first taken round by the parochial clergy. Typhus fever raged in Cork, and "fever in Ireland, not only at that time, but for many a year before and for many a year after, was more like a plague than anything else." S. A. describes the condition of the towns in the early part of this century as truly horrible, from the insanitary state of the poorer streets, and the extreme poverty of the inhabitants. Whether the disease were typhus or typhoid fever — whether it were actually contagious or epidemic—matters little. "There was no great difference except in terms: attendance on fever cases was highly dangerous to doctors, priests, nuns, and all generally. Before the winter was out two of the 'walking nuns' caught the infection. The first one was ill twenty-one days before the crisis came. She was not convalescent when the second caught the same disease, which caused a relapse to the first patient. As the nuns were now only five in all, Mrs Aikenhead having been obliged to resume her post in Dublin, the terrible distress of the other three may be faintly imagined. Mrs Teeling, who had been left as rectress, attended to the sick nuns, with a lay-nurse as assistant, and the others spent their days among the poor, and helped to watch at night." The two doctors, who were father and son, gave their services for nothing, and the younger went to the chemist and to market for the community. The first Sister who fell ill recovered, the second patient, who was a younger sister of Mrs Aikenhead's own, fell into consumption, and having been recalled to Dublin, died in Stanhope Street about eighteen months later on.

Through this time of great distress the little community held on firmly, new members joined them, and their work rapidly increased. If a bed were not immediately forthcoming for a new arrival, she slept on blankets doubled up on the floor. "The Sisters of Charity were not too particular. They could put up with a great deal of inconvenience, even while going through an immense amount of anxious toil." There were times when they had a difficulty in providing their own food, and when they were forced to visit the poor without a penny to give them. "On one occasion the Superior and another Sister set out on their visitation with only three-halfpence in their pocket. In downright anguish of mind they went to innumerable sick and destitute people, giving them nothing but kind words and promises and prayers. At length they reached a house where a family were sheltering who had been evicted from their little holding. The father was lying sick unto death with his starving children around him. The little ones came peeping into the nuns' basket, hoping for something. The Superior gathered them round her and prayed, and told them she had come unprepared, and had given away all she had, but that she would return in the morning and bring them food. As she went out she told her companion with tears that this was the first time she felt her vow of poverty almost too heavy; but that she hoped in God." In the morning came £10 in a letter with the superscription, "For the poor of Christ." And this anonymous donor kept up a series of gifts, which amounted to a regular annual income of £100, for thirty years.

The Sisters of Charity, who thus struggled on through poverty and fever in 1828, have now six houses in Cork and its immediate vicinity.

Meanwhile, Mary Aikenhead herself having returned to Dublin, one work after another was added to those already in full swing—works which must perforce be passed over in these pages—till we come to the year 1832, and the first appearance of cholera. In Ireland, Dublin was the first place attacked, and cases were reported on the 22nd of March. The Penitentiary at Grange-Gorman, close to Stanhope Street, was converted into a cholera hospital, and the Sisters were sent in by desire of the Archbishop. It seems to have been the first time they had been called upon to face cases of pestilence collected in wards, and equally it was the first time that doctors, in such an emergency, had found themselves able to rely upon "walking nuns."

So frightful was the mortality that a Sister counted eight different occupants of one bed in the course of twenty-four hours. Among the nurses the loss was also frightful. The poor women who acted in that capacity—many of them not the most sober or respectable characters in the city—came in at night to attend the sick, and before morning it frequently happened that they were all carried out among the dead. Every morning a list of the dead was posted at the hospital gates, and usually numbered from fifty to eighty names. The Sisters went at eight in the morning, and, with a short interval for dinner and another for meditation, as one by one they could be spared, they remained in the wards till nightfall. Some of them were novices, for the supply of professed Sisters was but scanty in 1832, but they went into danger as young soldiers into battle. "Only one of the Sisters took the contagion. She had been for some time attending the hospital, when one morning the sad news reached her that her mother had just died of cholera. The Sisters besought her not to go that day to the wards, but she, thinking that a season of public calamity was not a time for the indulgence of personal sorrow, prevailed on the Superior to allow her to go to her post as usual. By-and-by, she was seized with the first symptoms of the disease and strove, but of course vainly, to contend against the enemy. She was soon laid prostrate, and a sad procession was seen approaching the Convent, three of the doctors bringing home their indefatigable ally, Sister Mary Francis. She got over the attack, and in a few days was in the hospital attending to the patients as usual."

We must hasten on to the foundation which perhaps of all others made the Order of Charity a real permanent power in Dublin—that of St Vincent's Hospital in St Stephen's Green. Vividly does the writer of these lines remember the first visit paid there in the autumn of 1861,—the sitting, on a Sunday morning, in a parlour of what had once been the splendid town house of the Earls of Meath, and a never-forgotten conversation with a nun. St Vincent's had then been in full activity for more than twenty years. It was a tremendous piece of work to undertake, and involved the sending over of three of the Sisters to be trained at the hospital of La Pitié in Paris. We must remember that in the thirties the whole of the nursing movement so familiar to our English ears was absolutely unthought of. These three Irish ladies set off on an unknown mission, and we gather that Mrs Aikenhead had more difficulty in persuading the charitable public of the wisdom of starting a hospital under trained nurses than of any other work she had previously undertaken. But the French were quite used to the idea, and the Filles de St Thomas had forty houses throughout France, most of them attached to hospitals.

The first money which came in for the establishment of St Vincent's was a gift of £3000 from Sister Mary Teresa O'Ferrall. It was applied to the purchase of the aforesaid premises in Stephen's Green, the town house of the Earls of Meath, just then offered for sale; and a struggle ensued to provide funds for the start. We hear first of a few pounds being given for the purchase of linen, and how Mrs Aikenhead made the bolster and pillow-slips with her own hands, while lying invalided from overwork in Sandymount, and then of the difficulties of fitting up the great old house with wards for the sick, and cells for the Sisters, and of establishing their own private chapel, where mass was to be said on Sundays and holy days. It is impossible to pursue the details at any length; it was several years before the next house to Lord Meath's was also offered for sale, and was secured by the order,—years before St Vincent's assumed the form and size it possessed when first I myself saw it, now thirty-seven years ago, but time steadily brought increase of strength and added means. Nor did the foundation of another great city hospital take anything from St Vincent's. "The Catholic heart was large enough to embrace both." My task in regard to this one first work is sufficiently accomplished if I can indicate to others that open doorway where I myself received one of the chief lessons of my own life.

It is almost time to return to Mary Aikenhead herself, and to note the incidents of her personal career. We have seen her in her gay youth at Cork, and in her first efforts to help Mrs John O'Brien in works of charity; we have seen her starting under the care of Dr Murray for the Bar Convent at York in 1812, at the age of twenty-five, and returning to Dublin a professed nun in the Waterloo year. We have found her with Mother Catherine, organising the first small conventual home in North William Street (William of Orange left his mark in Dublin in more places than one!), and then leaving Mother Catherine there, and moving herself to Stanhope Street on its green hill, once really a country site, and a fine locality for the great move. It is indeed a consecrated place to this generation, trodden by the unresting feet of the foundress, and her first group of assistant nuns. S. A. remarks on its small size, but the rooms are such in proportion and height, as are now by one of those refluxes of taste of which we have seen so much during the last forty years in England, just the "right thing" in domestic architecture. I have sat for hours in its parlour, under circumstances which have stamped its every line into my heart and imagination, and make vivid by contrast that cold and dreary evening in January 1819, when Mrs John O'Brien drove up in her carriage taking Mary Aikenhead and one other Sister, Mrs O'Reilly, to sleep there for the first time, with the three young women to act as servants, two of whom became lay Sisters. The great convent and the beautiful church which now stands close to that "small house" were dreams of the future, and the garden, now so neat and blooming, was all upset by the first building operations. Fifty years later, on the 2nd of February 1869, Stanhope Street Convent celebrated its jubilee. Mary Aikenhead was dead, but Mrs John O'Brien was still living, past eighty years of age, and the then Mother-General and all the older members of the Dublin House came up that steep hill, and great were the festivities among the children and the poor, who were served by the Sisters. The first stone of the present church was laid a year later, on St Augustine's Day, 1870, a memorable day in the neighbouring country of France, for the German armies were gathering between the frontier and Paris, and the work of wholesale destruction was begun. In Ireland the ever-living, ever-re-creating power of faith was celebrating half-a-century of fruitful work for God and man. Less than a year later Mrs John O'Brien passed away—a death which must be recorded in S. A.'s own words.

"While the building of the church was going on, the institution lost three of its greatest friends and benefactors. The first of these was Mrs John O'Brien, the founder, we may say, of the Stanhope Street Home of Refuge, or, as it is now called, St Mary's Industrial Training School. Mrs O'Brien had reached the venerable age of eighty-six years, when she died on the 28th of March 1871. During the last two years of her life her clear intellect became somewhat impaired, but her mind, when it wandered, revisited the old scenes. She would often order her carriage and want to get ready to attend the committee meetings at the Refuge, and when she was able to go out, and the servant would ask where he was to drive she was sure to say 'to Stanhope Street.' 'Our community,' say the annals of the Convent, 'looks upon it as a particular interposition of Providence that it fell to the lot of the Sisters of this home to attend to our dear friend and benefactress during her last days on earth, and that by special permission we were allowed to remain with her during the last three days of her holy life. We had the honour to receive her last sigh and the comfort to close her eyes and arrange her holy remains in the habit of a Dominican of the third order, to which she belonged for many years, R.I.P. Her great and generous acts must have soon obtained for her the vision of God, but our deep feelings of gratitude to our first and greatest benefactress could not be satisfied without a monthly mass, which is said regularly in our convent chapel for her eternal repose.'"

It is again more than a quarter of a century since the jubilee of the Convent at Stanhope Street, and from the novitiate which may practically be said to date from thence, have gone forth workers to all parts of Ireland. There are six houses of Sisters of Charity in Cork and its neighbourhood alone; there are asylums of various kinds, schools, a factory in County Mayo, and most familiar of all to me, the noble Hospice for the Dying at Harold's Cross.

CHAPTER II

THE HEAT OF THE DAY

WHEN Mary Aikenhead returned from York, at the age of twenty-five, we must picture to ourselves a tall, fine-looking woman, with dark eyes and plenty of physical vigour. It was much needed, for though young people started up to help her, and eagerly gave themselves to the novitiate, the work increased on every side. One young novice caught a fever and died; more than one failed from delicacy of health. "At North William Street, Mrs Aikenhead had filled many posts—managed the home as Superior, went abroad to visit the sick, and often cooked the dinner. On two days a week it did not take much cooking, being nothing but oatmeal porridge. One day, when Mrs Aikenhead found herself alone in the house, she thought it a good opportunity for scouring the stairs. She was in the midst of this work, with her sleeves turned up, her long skirt pinned, and a capacious checked apron covering her habit, when a ring at the bell summoned her from the pail! A right reverend prelate asked if the Superior were at home. Mrs Aikenhead ushered him into the parlour, saying the reverend Mother would be with him presently. He did not recognise the hard-working serving Sister in the dignified and elegant Mother Superior, who shortly appeared at his side."

But the incessant work and responsibility told early upon her. For a month previous to the death of the Sister (Mary Teresa Lynch) who had caught fever, Mrs Aikenhead sat up with her every night, and in 1818 she herself fell ill for the first time, and had to be carried off for two hot months of the summer to a country house of Dr Ball's. It was on her return in September that the Refuge in Stanhope Street was handed over to her by the secular committee, and, as before described, Mrs Aikenhead went to live there four months later; and for seven years she devoted herself to training the steadily increasing congregation, and actively aiding and superintending the multifarious duties of visiting nuns. These years were for the devoted woman the last years of health. At forty years of age incessant labour of body and brain left her physically disabled. The immediate disease was spinal inflammation, for which she was treated with the violent old remedies of that time. She was actually dosed "experimentally" for internal cancer, "a disease which she had not, and this proceeding would probably have proved fatal to life but for the interference of the apothecary, who came to the nuns and said: 'Ladies, you may get anyone to make up these medicines, I will have nothing to do with them; reverend Mother is being poisoned.' This good man was a great admirer of Mrs Aikenhead, who had, he said, 'a heart as big as the Rotunda, and a head to match.' He certainly did a good service by this vigorous protest. The doctor was changed, the real cause of the illness discovered, and a different line of treatment entered upon. The new doctor was Joseph Michael O'Ferrall, a young man who had already risen to some eminence in his profession." Mrs Aikenhead lived on to old age, but for some years was confined to her room and practically to her bed, nor could she ever again follow the duties of community life. But she never ceased working with her head and pen, and Dr O'Ferrall proved to her not only a skilful physician but a devoted ally. Nobody who follows the history of the many foundations made in different towns could imagine, were it not distinctly stated, that the plans were efficiently made and carried out by a stationary invalid. In the early thirties she was "virtually at the head of ten different houses, all engaged in important, varied, and absorbing works; but the most that she could personally do was to drive out occasionally to visit the convents in or near Dublin. She was never able to accomplish a journey to Cork after the year 1828, and she never saw her convents in Waterford, Clarinbridge, and Clonmel." Her intelligence and her memory grasped every detail once seen, and enabled her to plan and forecast that which she was never destined to behold, in a wonderful way. And S. A. finely says that "God had certainly greatly blessed her in this—that among those whom He had called to be Sisters of Charity were many women highly gifted by nature and grace, who imbibed her spirit in its very essence, and were able to carry out her intentions with an understanding heart, and an intelligence that was not found wanting in unforeseen and difficult circumstances."

Mrs Aikenhead found herself often obliged to nominate comparatively young Superiors to new foundations. The special qualifications for ruling a religious house do not depend on anything like rotation of age. If the new Home was in or near Dublin, she kept each rectress in close communication with herself; and to those at a distance she wrote incessantly, aiming to keep up the "fundamental spirit" by pouring out her "own thoughts as they were suggested by the circumstances brought under her notice." She felt a great sympathy for young Superiors, remembering her own early dread of being placed in authority when still quite young.

As St Teresa appears to be such a favourite saint with the outside world, here is a letter written to a new Superior frightened at her responsibilities, in which Mrs Aikenhead brings her in effectively.

"Do, my dear, exert the good sense with which God has blessed you, but, above all, exercise unlimited confidence in Him who will never allow you to be tried above your strength. Be assured of it, the alarm we sometimes feel at undertaking offices of importance arises not infrequently from self-love and pusillanimity. Do imitate St Teresa and *spit at the devil*, who is trying to terrify you. The arch-enemy knows your weak point and assails it. In the Holy Name, then, tell him to begone. Believe me, by trying to combat this point of self-love you will please the Divine Majesty more than by fasts and austerities. Some penance we must all do. In the Name of Him Who has called us to honour Him, take up the spiritual armour spoken of by St Paul, and proclaim against the enemies you have renounced in Baptism—the devil, the world, and the flesh—that you will fight the battle stoutly. The flesh is our own *self-love*; the world, in our regard as religious, is, for the most part, *human respect*; and the hoof of the wicked one, the tail of the serpent, will ever be discovered by the lowly-minded who petition with the Church for a *right understanding.*"

This " right understanding " passed into a household word in the congregation, and S. A. tells us that she perpetually urged her children to pray for it, and that the prayers were certainly answered. On another page we are told that nothing in the correspondence comes out more fully than Mrs Aikenhead's faith in prayer, and her devotion to its exercise. " In great things and in small she turns to prayer, and she is always begging the prayers of others." On one page we find her saying that she had been promised some very particular aid from another order, adding that "we have established unions of prayer and good works with dear old York, now in all its renewed increase of numbers and potencies." Also, the Sœurs Hospitalières de St Thomas, who had trained the three Irish Sisters destined for the commencement of St Vincent's, were linked with her children in this matter, and so were the French Sisters of Charity, whom she calls "the real ones"; and she adds, "Now, as I have great comfort from thinking of these holy unions, I tell you of them." And she says that she often thinks that nothing short of a miracle—"nay, many miracles"—can bring in the number of novices required for supplying the necessary workers in the houses already founded.

For the work so laboriously started by the Foundress whose life we are considering, could not be carried out except by the free gift of many tens of other devoted lives. This is a point almost entirely ignored by those who fasten their minds on the utterances of some two or three saints, as if what they did for God could be explained by the sincerity and eloquence of their individual speech and writing. Saint Teresa roused a great wave of prayer, which has flowed on unslackened from her day to ours; "Monsieur Vincent" set agoing a great plan for nursing, serving, bed-making, cooking, which is in full activity now that two hundred years have passed away since the day when the old man of more than eighty died in his arm-chair. Dr Murray might have planned his new order for the needs of the poor in his native Ireland, and might have chosen one bright, courageous girl from another diocese to carry out his desire, but not a step could that good Bishop have advanced but for that great and divinely attractive Power which called soul after soul to give itself to the work. The management of great charities, the foundation of schools, the nursing of fevers and cholera, and all the ills which flesh is heir to, have never, since the modern world began, been carried out by all sorts of women, of all various ranks, for the unutterably foolish personal motives assigned to them by those who know nothing whatever about them. Mrs Aikenhead became, year by year, the commander of an ever-increasing troop, who were free conscripts of the army of the Lord; and she kept in touch with them through a most laborious pen. St Teresa said she was nearly "ground to powder" with writing letters, in days when the letters were probably tied up with silk and sent by a man on horseback. Mrs Aikenhead survived the establishment of the penny post by nineteen years. About fifteen hundred of her carefully begun and ended letters are preserved in the Mother House alone. How many of this particular group were read by S. A. during the writing of the biography my mind fails to imagine. From moral and practical advice bestowed on the heads of other subordinate groups, blended with expositions of the deeper things of Christian life, and descending from thence to the innumerable details of domestic existence in dwellings which were rated for taxation, and could never let out the kitchen fires,—what did not Mrs Aikenhead's pen achieve? And she was the centre in which all the others met. "She was careful to interest the Sisters in the work of various houses besides the one in which they themselves might happen to be more particularly engaged. The hospital nuns were not to nurse the idea that doctoring the poor was the foremost of all good deeds. The nuns of the schools were not to cultivate any bookish notions about the pre-eminence of their vocation. The nuns of the metropolitan laundry were not to set too high a value on washing. Town convents should not look on provincial houses as country cousins. As they were all ruled by the one head, so should they be all animated with the one spirit. Fortunately, she had that vital power of willing, and effecting what she willed, which enabled her to transfuse a truly fraternal spirit throughout her well-organised government."

Nor was she independent of the love and sympathy of others. She writes to the Mother Assistant, Mrs MacCarthy, who ultimately succeeded her, "I shall greatly enjoy a letter when you have the moments to write. But try to become a good intercessor, and come home to us with great stores of sanctity. Amen! You know that all you can tell me of what is good and happy among you, and especially the two dear Sisters, but still more specially that which will give comfort to their hearts, the well-being of dear, holy, and respected rev. Mother will be of interest. May our Lord bless you, dearest child. Pray for yours ever and affectionately in J. C.—M. A." The nun to whom this letter was written was a cousin of Cardinal Wiseman, whom she greatly resembled. It was my privilege once to be face to face with her, a few years after Mrs Aikenhead's death, during one of my first visits to Dublin.

Of the two young orphaned sisters who had been left to her care in her own early youth, one had married, the other, Anne Aikenhead, as related, had become a nun; and, being one of the five who had been sent to found the house in Cork in 1826, was also one of the two who were seized with typhus fever, which raged among the poor like a plague, and she finally died, at thirty. Alicia Clinch, in religion Mary Aloysius, who was the first attacked, recovered after a desperate illness, and, I believe, lived to old age. Another Miss Clinch, who worked for more than five-and-thirty years in the service of the poor, was nearly eighty when she died, and worked on to within three days of her very happy and holy death, "with an ardour which even age could not abate." Some were called early and some were called late; it made no difference to them.

The sister of Mary Aikenhead, who married a physician named Hickson, was early left a widow with three children, to whom the reverend Mother was a truly loving aunt. The boy grew up and entered the Austrian military service. One of the little daughters who had been placed at school at Princethorpe, in Warwickshire, became very delicate; and as Mrs Hickson was abroad with her son, Mrs Aikenhead sent for her niece and settled her at St Vincent's, in the convent part of the institution, that she might be under Dr O'Ferrall's intelligent care. One of the Sisters taught her, and everything possible was done for the sweet delicate little child. After many months of treatment she was restored to her mother; she lingered a while longer, and died when about fourteen years of age. This child-face flits across the page like that of a little angel visitant. She was remembered in the country house at Harold's Cross, where Mrs Aikenhead spent all her later years, as being "carried down to rev. Mother's room to have tea." A tender reminder of her own youth to the woman who had played so great a part in life, and whose affections rang true all round.

In trying to gather up the complicated story of so many arduous lives so as to interest those who cannot personally realise the families or the localities across that "salt estranging sea," it is necessary to detach special figures from the multitude of people grouped on S. A.'s magnificent canvas. In the book itself—a long large book, with ample notes—they fall into place like the personages in a great picture by Paul Veronese. It may be noted that those, few in number, who were ordained to die young were generally carried off by consumption. Sometimes, as in the case of Anne Aikenhead, the fatal disease was started by a fever caught by the bedside of the poor; sometimes, an ardent young soul wore out its earthly envelope prematurely. In the world, as in the religious life, there are brilliant and delicate natures who assuredly fulfil their own appointed task in their shortened lives, and of whom the pagan poet would have said, "Whom the gods love die young." But most of those who built up the first order of active unenclosed nuns in Ireland were long-lived people, resistant in body and brain. Outside the order the two great planners and supporters of the nascent Institution were Archbishop Murray and Mrs John O'Brien: they both lived to be well past four-score.

Dr Murray was close on eighty-four when his summons came in 1852. He had done a great work in his diocese; when he received his episcopal appointment there was not a decent place of Catholic worship within the walls of Dublin except the Church of St Teresa, lately erected in Clarendon Street; the chapels were hidden away in the "darkest and most loathsome lanes and alleys of the city." Before the Archbishop died, ninety-seven churches, great and small, had been erected in the diocese, at an expense of little less than £700,000. And each of these places of worship was a centre of devoted Christian labour. "In every parish many schools had been built by the people themselves at no small cost." The Schools of the Christian Brothers were in full swing; the Missionary College of All Hallows was founded, which has never ceased to send out young priests to other countries; three congregations of women had been founded by His Grace; and there were twenty-nine communities devoted principally to the care of the poor and the education of youth. Thirty years in the eighteenth century, and more than fifty in this one (now so rapidly drawing to its close), had Daniel Murray lived; and for close upon sixty years he had led the unresting life of a priest. His last public function was the office for the repose of the soul of Richard Lalor Shiel, the famous orator, who had died in Florence, and was to be buried in the family grave in Tipperary. The coffin had rested on the way in the Church of the Jesuit Fathers in Dublin. Dr Murray dined that night in his own house, the

Presbytery of the Cathedral Church in Marlborough Street. Next morning, Shrove Tuesday, he rose early to say his mass in his private oratory, and went down to the drawing-room for the altar wine. There, fortunately, he found his old friend, Mrs John O'Brien, who was herself getting on in years, and had the privilege of hearing the early mass said by Dr Murray. As he passed her she noticed that "he rubbed his hands in a peculiar way, and she asked—Was he in pain? He replied that he was, and at the same moment she saw his countenance change. Mrs O'Brien had just time to place a chair behind him when he sank into it, helplessly struck. For forty-eight hours the saintly old man lay in what appeared to be a stupor, and those who loved him were allowed to pass through the room, filled by the unceasing sound of prayer. Mrs O'Brien knelt like a statue at the side of the bed whereon he lay; and two Sisters of Charity knelt at the foot."

When at length, on Thursday, the second day of Lent, the change for death was seen to be coming on, one of the attendant priests "opening at once the Holy Gospels, commenced reading aloud the Passion from St John, while all others present threw themselves on their knees in supplication to heaven for the illustrious spirit hastening on its eternal path. After the lapse of some moments, to the amazement of them all, the archbishop was distinctly seen to raise under the bed-covering his right hand, which all through had been paralysed, and to move it, as if imparting his episcopal benediction to those around, and then passing it over his bosom, laid it tranquilly on his breast." So died the great priest, very poor in worldly goods; "the very house he lived in had been purchased for him by a few friends; even the common comforts of his daily life and the maintenance of a necessary establishment were looked to by personal friends." Whatever moneys came into his hands seemed " only to touch his hand for a blessing ere their distribution." Only one little saving is recorded. He loved the Refuge at Stanhope Street and St Vincent's Hospital, and among his effects was found a little box, sealed and directed, for Mrs Mary Aikenhead. This box contained 100 guineas.

She, to whom he had been as a father for forty years, was profoundly afflicted at his loss. She sent all her elder nuns to the house of mourning; she herself, always invalided, remained behind, weeping, and telling a young attendant, "My child, do not be disedified, nor imagine I am not perfectly conformed to God's holy will and divine ordination, but poor nature must have its way."

Mrs John O'Brien survived Dr Murray for nineteen years, and died at eighty-six, in March 1871, just at the time when the Commune had begun to devastate Paris—so close to our own time as to seem a link with three generations.

And one more member of what I will call the first quartette—Mother Catherine, who as Miss Alicia Walsh had accompanied Mary Aikenhead to be trained at the Bar Convent at York, died rather more than two years after Dr Murray. She also was quite an old woman, being fourteen years older than her companion, and nearly forty when she entered the religious life. She was born in 1773; her father was a man of considerable property in the county of Dublin, but upon the borders of Meath; her mother was a Taafe of a well-known Irish family despoiled in the Williamite wars. Mr and Mrs Walsh did not live to be old. "In the year 1798, Mr Walsh, though he took no active part in the insurrectionary movement, suffered, nevertheless, like many other Catholics, from the destruction of his property, which was pillaged and burnt by the Royalist soldiery." Alicia, their second daughter, a lively, affectionate, intellectual girl, threw herself into the cause of the prisoners, "going from prison to prison, at much personal risk, to carry messages from friends, or to console the inmates, who were the objects of her deepest sympathy." Of that terrible time she never would speak in after years. S. A. tells us that in her presence, at any rate, people *were* "afraid to speak of '98." But she recovered her nerve and elasticity, and when the two Irish ladies were received as postulants at York, it was the elder of the two who became the universal favourite; Mary Aikenhead was somewhat weighed down by the responsibility of having been chosen by Dr Murray as the future Superior of his new order. In religion, the latter took the name of Sister Mary Augustine, a name soon merged in that of "Rev. Mother," or "Mrs Aikenhead," and Alicia Walsh took the name of the Saint of Sienna, and when she got back to Dublin she became Mother Catherine for the rest of her days. The poor seldom spoke of her as Mrs Walsh, they caught at the other conventual name, and in the end she was so called by rich and poor alike. She played a great part in Dublin life; she was appointed Mother of Novices by Dr Murray, the day before the first postulant, Miss Catherine Lynch of Drogheda, was received (they came afterwards in plenty). When Mrs Aikenhead took over the lay Refuge of Stanhope Street from Mrs John O'Brien, Mother Catherine was left behind as Rectress at North William Street, with two other nuns, and one domestic candidate; and having gradually got possession of a few more novices and postulants sent them from Stanhope Street, Mother Catherine and a Sister began visiting the hospital in Jervis Street, the indefatigable Mrs John O'Brien accompanying them, apparently as a sort of protection in their quite new sphere of work. It may here be recalled that it was Mother Catherine who was sent with Mrs Aikenhead to attend at Kilmainham Gaol, when the two young women were condemned to death.

In 1830 Mother Catherine and her community were removed to the new convent in Gardiner Street, and the Church of St Francis Xavier gradually rose on an adjacent plot of ground. The great work which here engaged their attention was the care of the schools, and a bad time they had at the beginning; they were helped by a devoted Christian Brother, who seems to have been particularly small in stature, for, when he was first suggested by Mr Edmund Rice as a likely person to get the better of an unruly mob of children, the Sister of Charity, Mrs Hennessey, exclaimed, "Oh! that little boy?" "*Little boy!*" rejoined Mr Rice; "I wish I had fifty such *little boys*." So on Saturday, the only day on which small Brother Duggan was free, he appeared in the midst of a crowded room full of unruly children. He had to shout and whistle before he could command silence. But he succeeded in breaking in the wild colts, and so giving Mrs Hennessey such a practical lesson that, "for the rest of her life, she was such a finished schoolmistress that one would have thought she had never been anything else."

Two years later, Mother Catherine, who seemed always summoned the moment anything new and difficult or desperate was to be done, had to plunge with two of her community into the temporary cholera hospital. There she did the work which brought her into public notice, at least among the doctors. She was in her true element, and would not allow herself a moment's rest, though she was now close upon sixty years old. "As the hospital did not provide certain little luxuries which she considered might contribute to the comfort of the convalescent, she set out every morning with a basket under her nun's cloak, laden with supplies. She also took with her large lawn handkerchiefs to wipe off the ice-cold perspiration which exuded from the faces and hands of the agonising. In the evening she gathered these handkerchiefs, brought them home, washed them herself, so as to have them ready for the next day, nor would she allow anyone to do this for her, or to help her; no, there was no use in offering or entreating: Mother Catherine in this would have her way."

In Gardiner Street Mother Catherine lived and laboured for another twenty years. This convent, which long enjoyed the distinction of having the best schools, was also looked upon as the great mission-house of the congregation. The first Sister who offered herself for the Australian mission belonged here: her name was Sister Mary John Cahill; and when it was known in all the House that Archbishop Polding of Sydney, and his Vicar-General, Dr Ullathorne, had asked for nuns, and that the latter had written a pamphlet, describing the harrowing nature of the convict life in Australia, Mrs Cahill wrote to Mrs Aikenhead a letter, dated from Upper Gardiner Street, 27th of February 1838, and this was its tenour:—

"My Dear Rev. Mother,—If you think Almighty God would receive one so unworthy, I would be most willing to share the labours of the Australian mission. I am aware of my deficiencies, and still more of my want of virtue; but I trust that, if chosen by Him, He will prepare the instrument for His own work. He knows that I desire nothing but to fulfil His holy will. I have had this long time this good work at heart, and I often wished to accompany the wretched convicts on board to begin there what the insubordination in Newgate rendered so difficult. I would not presume to offer my poor

services for this holy work, but that 'the head cannot say to the feet I have no need of you.' As I believe that God enlightens Superiors in what regards the particular as well the general good of all, I expect to learn His holy will in this, as well as in all other concerns, through the medium of His representative.—With great respect, I remain, my dear reverend Mother, your obedient child in Christ,
SISTER MARY JOHN CAHILL."

Four other Sisters volunteered, one of whom was too delicate to be accepted; and a sixth, Mrs de Lacy, who had entered expressly for the Australian mission, and made her vows the previous year, joined the rest. Mrs Aikenhead gathered them to the Mother House in Stanhope Street, spared herself neither trouble nor fatigue, in spite of her invalid condition, and took care they should have every comfort and convenience she could procure. She gave furnishing for their own chapel, and all requisites for opening a school; she gave them a well-chosen collection of books, and, above all, she gave them prayers and blessings, and confided them to the care of Dr Ullathorne, who had come over to Europe. They sailed from Gravesend on the 18th of August 1838, and reached Sydney on the last day of the year. New South Wales was then a penal colony. It was the dreaded and detested "Botany Bay," so named by Captain Cook on account of its beautiful flowers! Even the poor convicts had a welcome for the nuns; and the Protestant Governor, Sir George Gipps, received them as friends, and harbingers of a better state of things. "One of the Sisters, looking back through the long vista of forty years to this period, said it would be difficult to describe the joy and gratitude of these poor souls as they welcomed the Sisters to their abode. Eight hundred women and three hundred children were confined in the prison. Their occupation was breaking stones and sawing wood!" But the Sisters had other and sadder people under their care. Listen to this: "Perhaps the dearest of all their duties was in the 'condemned cells.' The last survivor of the five emigrant Sisters (Sister Mary Baptist de Lacy, who returned to Ireland to die) had in her old age no sweeter remembrance of her labours of charity, multiform as they were, than this; and she told of many a beautiful death glorified by faith and hope and holy love, and the humility of a contrite heart, which was the lot not seldom of those who left the condemned cell, only to ascend the fatal platform."

If we seemed to have wandered away from Mother Catherine to follow one of her own special flock, the beauty of the story will atone. As she herself grew older—she was sixty-five when the Australians went away—she became a loving centre of universal help, and the account of her reminds one of the Parisian Sœur Rosalie in her old age. Mother Catherine had always a beautiful and engaging countenance. The young Alicia Walsh, who had hurried from prison to prison in '98, had become the old nun who found her way to every one's heart, rich and poor. Her sweet, calm manner never varied, even when a "holy zeal might seem to justify some warmth of expression." If people complained to her, she comforted them, and piloted them through their troubles. "One rich young man, who was commonly accused of parsimony, would come to Mother Catherine at dark and give her large sums—twenty or forty pounds, perhaps, for the poor. He would then ask the Mother's blessing; she would give it affectionately, and he would depart quite happy, and free from the embarrassment of human praise."

When she was ill the universal grief was inexpressible; when she got well the great doctor Sir Philip, who had been specially called in, said the improvement was a miracle; and the regular doctor replied, "Ah! if you only knew how many masses were offered for that woman!" She was very tender and motherly to her community. "One day a novice, who was under her care, came 'tearing downstairs,' as the children of the school would say, in anything but a nun-like fashion. 'Go up now, my child,' said Mother Catherine, 'and show me how a nice young novice who is keeping her rule would come downstairs.'" When the Sisters came in wet and weary from their visits to the poor, Mother Catherine would take off their wet cloaks and shoes and take them away to dry. She watched what they took in the way of food with solicitude, sending extra portions if she thought it necessary, as if she were a tender parent in the world. For the last few years of her life she was more or less of an invalid, having frequent though slight attacks of paralysis, which she herself did not realise. She attributed her little falls to some accident, and went about doing good as long as her feet would carry her. She failed much, and suffered much, towards the end; and about two months before her death it became necessary to appoint a new Rectress. "At first the dear sick Mother seemed greatly puzzled, and used to follow the newly-appointed Superior with her eyes, as if trying to find out what brought her to the house. The truth dawned on her one day, when she saw a Sister who was in the room rise on the entrance of the Rectress. As soon as the latter was near enough, Mother Catherine took her hand, kissed it, and bowed her head in token of obeisance. The new Rectress was thirty-two years her junior."

It was on Christmas morning, 1854, that Mother Catherine, the bright, ardent Alicia Walsh of the penal times, breathed her last, surrounded by her loving community; the prayers for the dying were finished, and the Passion of our Lord according to St John was being read as she passed away. She had always expressed a particular wish to die on Christmas Day. She was half-way through her eighty-second year; forty-two of those years had been spent in the religious habit, assumed in that old English convent at York. She had survived Archbishop Murray by two years; and she must have left a singular void in the associations of Mrs

HISTORIC NUNS

Aikenhead, whose first companion she had been. The great affection of the Dublin people linked their names constantly together,—the reverend Mother of the whole Order of Charity, and Catherine, the Mother of the poor.

Chapter III

1845. HAROLD'S CROSS

We must retrace somewhat to take up the thread of Mrs Aikenhead's own life. She was destined to survive Mother Catherine by some years, but these years were not spent at St Vincent's Hospital. She had there been brought into close relation with all classes in Dublin, and was a large and generous employer of labour, prompt and upright in all her business relations. An unresting stream of visitors came daily to those upper rooms, where the invalid Mother dwelt, and exercised an unrelaxing superintendence. Year after year passed by, and to her usual extreme feebleness of health was added the recurrent distress of bronchitis. It was then decided to move her into a beautiful old suburb of Dublin, to a house at Harold's Cross, purchased from a family belonging to the Society of Friends; and thus it was that Our Lady's Mount was first inaugurated. After the lapse of another half-century that small estate shelters one of the most beautiful charities in the world—the Hospice for the Dying.

When the house was bought, Mrs Aikenhead was fifty-seven years old; it was her destined home for the rest of her earthly days. The privilege of being the Mother House, hitherto enjoyed by Stanhope Street, was now transferred to Harold's Cross; the novitiate was moved thither so that the young postulants, who had been lodged temporarily at St Vincent's, were again gathered under Mrs Aikenhead's wing, and she was able from her invalid chamber to superintend the character and development of each new subject. The houses to which the novices were drafted off after profession were already many. To Stanhope Street had been successively added Gardiner Street, St Vincent's in Stephen's Green, Sandymount. In Cork was a vigorous though much-tried offshoot (there are now six houses in the southern city and its vicinity), and Waterford had followed suit. In a few years, the Waterford Convent, with its numerous annexes, became one of the most important and interesting houses of the congregation. The Bishop had applied for nuns, and a native of the town, Miss Christian Quan, who was unable, for domestic reasons, to herself take the vows, had helped by saving up money and by making personal exertion, in the successful planting of the new house. Another Miss Quan was a member of the Community in Cork.

Then the Australian Mission, already detailed, had been organised in 1838, and the convent at Clonmel opened in the same year in which the reverend Mother moved to Harold's Cross. Clarinbridge, in County Galway, was already a year old. Ten houses, each carrying out several works, such as nursing the sick, keeping large schools, sheltering penitents, looking after young girls (many hundreds gradually being aggregated in every locality), and widespread visiting of the poor. All this multifarious work had been planned and cherished and governed by the sick woman, who mounted with difficulty the broad low staircase of that old house in Harold's Cross in 1845. I am not compiling a list or dictionary or a blue-book. The facts are told with extraordinary eloquence by S. A., and are noted down for many successive years after Mrs Aikenhead's death—indeed, up to 1880. But my own knowledge began to be accumulated twenty years before that, and will soon have covered the long space of forty years. I want my readers to see with the mind's eye that which I myself have seen and known.

The view from the house at Harold's Cross is a little altered from what it was when Mrs Aikenhead took possession of it. The "square, sufficiently large, but not very lofty room on the second storey" (meaning the one above the entrance), has still its "two windows, rather broad than high, which looked out on the green tree-dotted lawn, with a pond at the end." It has still a third window on the west side, and close to the other, which then looked into a "spacious garden, well stocked with hardy fruit-trees, fragrant, but by no means rare flowers, and vegetables of every sort and size." But part of that spacious garden, spreading right up to the fields, has since been given up to the beautiful building now called Our Lady's Hospice for the Dying, in front of which is a gravelled space, bordered by ample turf and flower-beds; and from the end of the long upper corridor of that Hospice is still that great open western view, flat and fully-cultivated, with a fringe of trees about a distant village. A garden-path winds round the end of the building into the remainder of the spacious garden, still full of roses; and herein is the mortuary chapel. The pond is where it was, and the trees are thick around it, although the row of poplars has been cut down; and I made the discovery last August that this pond must be supplied from the Liffey, for the tide rises and falls.

Here, from 1845 onward, dwelt Mrs Mary Aikenhead, with the junior members of the congregation constantly around her. Her health was improved by the country air, and having only one low flight of stairs to descend, she could get into a bath-chair and be taken all over the pretty grounds: sometimes she would write her notes out-of-doors. It was a great and beneficent change after the eleven years spent on the top storey of the Hospital in Dublin, though that enjoys the great space of Stephen's Green.

As old age crept on, her admiration for the beauties of nature seemed to increase rather than diminish. She had never really lived in the country before, and though many of her convents were founded in interesting and picturesque localities, she had been too busy in her younger days to dwell on their outward charms; and several of them in distant parts of Ireland she had literally never seen, though she had minutely directed their ways and works. But "now in the garden and the fields she had wherewithal to delight her pious and poetic mind." She loved her garden flowers, and the younger nuns carried them up to her. "It was most animating," said one who knew her well, "to hear her praising the beauties of a flower; for which reason her children vied with one another in having flowers to present to her, so that they might hear the grandeur of her praises of the Great Creator." "For many years it was her habit to watch the setting sun; and even in old age she would have her chair placed near a window whence she could have a good view of the 'glorious sun,' as she would say; and while watching the silver and golden clouds until they had disappeared, she would utter the most exalted sentiments of praise and prayer, and exclaim: 'What must be the glory of heaven!'"

She grew old beautifully. A lady went to see her who afterwards joined the order; and wrote: "When I first went to her on this errand, she could walk a little. So she came downstairs assisted by a lay sister, leaning on a stick, and attended by a very plebeian black dog, which leaped up behind her when she sat down, and made one of the party. 'This is Dandy,' she said, 'my faithful dog.' I took greatly to the idea of the dog, and thought there was a promise of kindness in the fact of his being admitted to the friendship of the Mother of the congregation. She struck me as a magnificent old woman, with—I cannot say the remains of great beauty, but—a beauty remarkable of its kind. There was a grandeur in the outline of the features and in their expression; and there were certain curves about the mouth and cheeks which I do not remember to have seen so marked in any other face. Her large, well-set eyes, which looked soft enough to melt when she was moved, and were so heavenly when a holy chord was touched, had also much humour in them at times, and could give full expression to a majestic severity when it was necessary to defend a just cause. Her soul shone through them.

"My first impressions were confirmed by further experience. She inspired both fear and love. But the fear was, perhaps, rather that diffidence which one feels in the presence of a powerful and strongly individualised character. And yet, I do not remember that I ever met anyone to whom I approached with greater confidence, and in whose presence I less felt my own weakness. I heard another person say the same thing; a woman of the world, very intellectual, by no means pious in the sense in which the word is usually taken, and with faults plain enough to be seen. This lady had mixed much with clever people, and had a reputation for talent, but in the presence of the reverend Mother she was a child —and a good child.

"I often noticed the effect she produced on people of the world. It was a right good effect. She was most agreeable in manner, and full of information. She commanded respect, and instinctively people came out in their best aspect when in her presence.

"Like all great minds, she was open to expostulation and advice, and could humble herself instantaneously. One time she was sending a severe message to some offender by a dear and trusted Sister, who acted for her in a thousand cases when she was herself unable to go about. The sister said: 'Dear Mother, I cannot give that message.' 'Why, my heart?' 'Oh, it would do harm,' she answered; 'let me say it in my own way,' and then explained how. Reverend Mother paused, and then said, quietly and humbly: 'Say, my dear, whatever the Holy Ghost will inspire you to say.' On another occasion she had reprimanded a Sister whose impetuosity had carried her too far. Another Sister came in and found the delinquent in tears by the side of reverend Mother, who said: 'Here am I, combing my child's hair with a three-legged stool!' and taking her into her great arms, she gave her an embrace that set all right in a moment. She was far from implacable, and a small thing would divert her from her momentary severity."

This is, perhaps, the fitting place in which to record another trait of Mary Aikenhead's character —its singular magnanimity and single-eyed devotion to the interests of her Master and His Church. The story of the Institute of the Sisters of Mercy will be told in the succeeding section of this book, and as it was partly contemporaneous with the prior Institute, it necessarily touched upon a sphere which for many years had exclusively been occupied by the earlier congregation. The one was about fifteen years earlier in its actual foundation, and much more than that if the long time of planning by the Archbishop, and the training of the postulants at

York be taken into account. But, unfortunately, "the two institutes became the subject of comparison and contrast; and a rivalry, which was never contemplated by the admirable women who were at the head of these congregations, was well-nigh established by injudicious partisans in the outside rank." These are the words of one who never made a superfluous remark. It seems as if in that great outburst of faith and charity, which swept over Ireland in the first half of this century, the Bishops themselves sometimes hesitated on which congregation to rely for a given work, where both were so devoted and efficient. And on one occasion Mrs Aikenhead took up her pen and wrote very noble words to the Superior of one of her own convents, whose projected undertaking—a hospital—"seemed likely to be given over by the Bishop of the diocese" to the other nuns.

"Let us take care of every illusion of false zeal or false love of our own institute. Both are intended for the same great end of promoting the glory of our Heavenly Father and the good of the poor. We cannot promote either if charity does not reign in our hearts. All other feelings merge in self; and miserable earthly preference for self will banish the divine spirit from us. Let us remember that no effort of human exertion could succeed in forming their institute if God had not assisted; and should we presume to wish His favours to be confined only to ourselves? Our efforts must be to deserve the fullest measure of the divine blessing on our congregation and the good works entrusted to our care; but would it be like the children of the God of *infinite love* to allow corrupt nature to grow rebellious in our hearts, so as to repine that others, equally His children, and redeemed by His precious blood, should also be made the chosen instruments of His mercy to the poor and afflicted ? Look into the sentiment, and see how unworthy it is of our high vocation. . . ."

In another letter, alluding to feelings of outside friends, she says : " Whatever remarks are heard in the parlour should be listened to with reserve, and nothing should urge us to give an opinion. Perhaps this rising congregation may be far more pleasing in the divine sight than our own."

This is a fine utterance from the woman who had borne the burden and the heat of the earlier day, when an active order of nuns was a thing unknown in Ireland, and even in the British Isles. The steadiness and strict concentration of the Order of Charity had provoked criticism as compared to the rapid spread of the Order of Mercy. But Dr Murray and his selected helper knew what they wanted from the first, and their united work stands solid as a rock ; and its brave affectionate Founders welcomed every new labourer under whatever sacred badge, saying : " There will be all the beauty and ornament of variety ; and may we emulate the glorious privilege of being interwoven and worthy branches, or even sweet flowers of the holy garland which is to decorate the dear Island of Saints."

Page after page might be extracted revealing the different aspects of Mary Aikenhead's character ; and, indeed, to its deeper and more spiritual side very little reference has been made. Lying on a sick-bed for months at a time, and for nearly thirty years governing the different houses of the order very largely by her pen, she was unwearying, not only in practical advice, but in spiritual support and consolations to the younger Superiors at a distance. It was her happy lot to be ably seconded by them, and in all her correspondence there is evidence, not only of her own strong sense and intellectual culture, but also of similar qualities in those whom she addressed. Herein is ample and convincing evidence of the preposterous nature of the mental image formed by the outside public (and especially if they happen to be poets) of a nun. Certain of the printed letters are addressed to Mrs MacCarthy, who ultimately succeeded as Mother-General. It was she who was first cousin to Cardinal Wiseman, their mothers being sisters, and he was much attached to her. From the marked resemblance between the cousins, they might almost have been taken for twins. Both faces were plain, and strongly marked by sense and kindness.

For about five years Mrs Aikenhead survived the two chief friends and supporters of her youth. Only Mrs John O'Brien remained to her; but at Harold's Cross an active flourishing community grew up round her. She seems to have attained the age of seventy without much worsening of her usual infirm state, which had always left her the power of writing freely and governing energetically. But in her seventy-second year her bodily frame gave way, and for many months the beloved old Mother-General drew failing breath in the great arm-chair, which still stands in the room already described—the room with the three windows, one of which now commands the great new building which shelters one hundred dying people. This was built long after Mary Aikenhead's own death in 1859, but is the direct fruit of her life and her labours. And not only at Harold's Cross, but in many other places, new buildings, housing new charities, have sprung up, erected by her daughters in religion, and served by them. At Foxford, in County Mayo, is a woollen mill planted upon the rocks of a most desolate district, but in close neighbourhood of water power. This convent, and the refuge opened near Liverpool, are the last of the new foundations of which I happen to have heard; but I do not want to burden my book with statistics, and I have not been able to get across the rocks, large and little, between Harold's Cross and County Mayo—that pilgrimage must be for younger feet. I have tried to tell shortly the story of those earlier years of the century, when an old Bishop and a young woman of five-and-twenty roused themselves to lift up the poor of their race from sorrows and indignities which it is useless now to recall—years when Daniel Murray and Mary Aikenhead stood out as evangelists of an applied Gospel, and heralds of a better time. They were fervent, indeed, but it was not only fervour which did that work. Two hundred years earlier they might have laid their devoted heads upon the block. One hundred years earlier they would have laboured silently by prayer; but the moment had come, in 1812, when another method could bear fruit, and these two together achieved a great result, by a rare blending of faith and sense and statesmanship, in which the woman bore her full part for more than forty years as the coadjutor of the man. The Order of Charity is an integral part of the real administration of Ireland. Its foundations are to be counted by twenties, its workers by hundreds; and Dr Murray and Mary Aikenhead were pioneers of a great revival, which puts our unhappy attempts at legislation to shame.

CATHERINE M'AULAY

In Baggot Street, Dublin, is a large house whose corridors may be said to lead to the ends of the earth, with unnumbered forks and branches touching every colony and every English-speaking state; and in that house abides a great memory: that of a woman who did not live to be aged, neither had she found her definite vocation in the days of her youth, but who, in fifteen years, laid the firm basis of the great Order of Mercy, and then laid herself down to die, worn out with work.

Catherine M'Aulay belonged to a well-connected and well-endowed family, Catholic in creed, but exposed to varying influences in days when the social politics of Ireland weighed heavily against the faith of the people. Her father was a strict and devout man; her mother an affectionate and brilliant woman, who disliked what she considered the vulgar associations connected with her husband's apostolic work among the poor. The wealthier Catholics found themselves in a condition of social ostracism which was hard to bear. The only recollection Catherine retained of her early childhood referred to a remonstrance made by her mother to her father on his habit of gathering a crowd of his poorer neighbours for instruction in the hall of his large house, or, in warm weather, upon the lawn. "She besought him in accents of terrible reproach to desist from an occupation so unbecoming to his character and position. Mrs M'Aulay was quite willing to be a Lady Bountiful among the poor: she was beautiful and amiable, fond of gaieties, and harmonious in temper; but she did not like her "house to become a receptacle for every beggar and cripple in the country." Her little daughter, destined to become one of those winning personalities before whom obstacles fall and helpers arise on every hand, combined the qualities of both parents. She was only seven years old when the father died, and his widow possessed little knowledge of business. Her pecuniary affairs became unsettled, and she was advised to sell Stormanton House, a great place, where she had passed her married life, and remove to Dublin. But the estate was slow in finding a purchaser, a report having arisen that the house was haunted—people evidently remembered that in "the troubled times" a murder had been committed in the garden. Nothing supernatural had ever been reported of the premises in Mr M'Aulay's time; but, now that his widow wanted to sell the property, it became difficult to find a purchaser. At last a sale was effected, and the old homestead passed away finally from the family; and when, twenty years later, Catherine become an heiress, was urged by her brother to repurchase it, she invariably replied that she regarded herself as steward, not as owner, of the wealth she had inherited.

In Dublin, therefore, she received her education, and amidst very mixed influences. Her mother contracted an intimacy with a Mrs St George, widow of an officer in the British army, a lady of a "literary turn of mind, and quite remarkable for the grace and elegance of her manners." The children became fond of her, and in this very unspiritual atmosphere the child who was to do so much for the Kingdom of God passed the next few years. But Mrs M'Aulay did not long survive her husband; she died when Catherine was about eleven years old, attended by a priest of her own faith, but having made no arrangement for the children remaining in the hands of Catholic guardians. To the end of her own life, Catherine M'Aulay retained a most painful memory of this deathbed scene; of her mother's remorse for her own worldly indifference, and the lapse into insensibility which rendered all discussion about the future of her children impossible. The poor lady died, and the orphans were handed over to a relative, Surgeon Conway, a rigid Protestant, kind and good to them according to his lights, but a man who would have thought it "a vulgarity and a species of disloyalty to mention Catholicity in his fashionable and well-regulated mansion." He managed to keep his young charges aloof from everything which could remind them of the faith of their own parents. Catherine did not know a single Catholic, and there was nothing in the streets of the city to indicate the existence of a Catholic church, neither steeples nor bells, these being only allowed on edifices by law established. The little girl retained a fixed and determined attitude with regard to public worship, and, not being allowed to go to mass, she went nowhere.

Surgeon Conway, from having been a rich man, became a poor one. We are not told how this happened, but it did not alter Catherine's position in regard to his family, and when, at sixteen, she had "several opportunities" of forming an eligible marriage, she rejected them all; she did not want to marry, and her intense nature centred itself in endeavours to get instruction in her father's religion. Just about this time a lady and gentleman, distantly connected with her mother, returned to Ireland from India. They purchased Coolock House, an estate a few miles north of Dublin. This childless couple, struck with Catherine's attractive charm, offered to adopt her, and, naturally, the arrangement was too advantageous to be refused by her guardian. Catherine went to live with Mr and Mrs Callahan as their adopted child, and the whole course of her life was changed. This happened in 1803.

Mr Callahan was much easier to live with than Surgeon Conway. A clear picture is obtainable of him as a kind-hearted, intelligent survivor of the intellectual eighteenth century. He had a strong scientific turn, and never attended any place of worship. He was very kind and affectionate to his wife, whose health had been injured in India. Although a Quakeress by birth, we are told that she very rarely went to meeting, and that she regarded

Mr Callahan "with mingled feelings of admiration and respect." She was certainly a worthy partner of his best feelings and intentions, for we are told how she forgave a miserable young man who had cruelly insulted her by anonymous letters, and, after a sharp interior struggle, she persuaded her husband to procure for him a commission in the army, and burnt the letters which had caused her so much pain. The story is wrapped up in mystery. The young man was a distant cousin, and presumably jealous of Miss M'Aulay's position as an adopted child. In any case, he was a veritable snake in the grass.

We are next told that Surgeon Conway's only daughter ran away from home, and contracted a marriage beneath her own station in life. The union proved very unhappy, and Catherine ultimately become the providence of the poor woman and her children. Two of these eventually became Sisters of Mercy.

Of the years of Catherine's young womanhood there is not much record. She lived as a young lady in the home of rich parents, practising her religion more and more openly as she grew older. Her brother and sister, having been brought up as Protestants, remained so. The latter, when very young, married Dr William M'Aulay, a physician of some eminence, and probably a cousin. The brother, James M'Aulay, entered a military academy, where in course of time he graduated with honour. He became surgeon and staff officer, served several campaigns under Sir Arthur Wellesley, and, after Waterloo, retired from the army and practised as a physician in Dublin. In politics he was "just such another Irishman as his Commander-in-Chief." The two brothers-in-law, James and William, were fond of wrangling about religion, or rather (as they themselves agreed) of descanting on topics very disagreeable to Catherine, who usually remained silent, while her gentle sister Mary, who would not willingly give pain, remonstrated with husband and brother. "They forgot that Kittie was a Catholic." But Kittie kept her love for both of them, and in later years the children of William and Mary M'Aulay became her dearest charges, and some of them helped in her own work.

When Miss M'Aulay was somewhat past thirty, her adopted mother was affected by severe sickness, and for the last two years never left her room. Her eyes grew so weak that she could not bear the least glimmer of light, and her filial nurse was obliged to sit in almost perpetual twilight, reading by a shaded light when Mrs Callahan was asleep. Mr Callahan became troubled at Kittie's careworn looks, and asked her if there was nothing she wanted. He could not reconcile himself to seeing the handsome accomplished daughter of his adoption leading so secluded and monotonous a life. "One day he asked her if there was anything on earth she wished for? She replied there was not, unless it were the means of doing more good among the poor.

"'But if I were to die, Kittie, what would you then do? You don't seem inclined to accept any matrimonial offer.'

She told him she had not thought of that contingency, but was sure that in any case God would take care of her.

"'But would you not like to be very rich?' persisted the old gentleman.

"'Whatever God pleases, Mr Callahan,' was the quiet reply."

Then one day he suggested that, as her adopted father, he had a right to know what she intended to do with herself after his death. He was merely trying to find out whether there was any truth in the report that she intended to become a nun.

There now occurred certain changes in the little family which, from what may be found in biographies, were not very uncommon in Ireland, which is enveloped in a concentrated atmosphere of prayer. Both of the good people who had nurtured the orphan girl, after a life determinedly opposed to the faith of the people, became Catholics before they died. Mrs Callahan was attacked by wearing disease, and was subject to many fears, but these seemed to be connected with her human affections only. She was "haunted with the fear that her friends would tire of her." Yet the poor husband's affections for the wife of his youth never waned, and Catherine was unwearied in her love and service. We are told that Mrs Callahan "belonged to a sect which has given some illustrious converts to the Church, but perhaps fewer in proportion than any other." That sect being the Society of Friends, it is implied that she had never received baptism. And she seems to have been educated in the belief that Catholicism was a vulgar superstition, and the chapels, then few and small, fit as meeting-houses for "servants and beggars." How she came round, received baptism, and died not many days afterwards, is a story too long to quote. Her one remaining fear was that Mr Callahan might make it a plea for ruining Catherine's prospects in life, and she would not have him told. She had been married very young, and died at sixty-five, after fifty years of conjugal life. Mr Callahan who was, naturally, several years older, was miserably shaken by the loss of his companion. He was, indeed, past eighty, and when pressed to consult new physicians he replied that he knew enough of their science to be certain that his case was beyond their skill. We gather that he belonged nominally to the English Church (to speak clearly), for he had a friend in the rector of a neighbouring parish; but he was not in the least pious, seldom went to any place of worship, "and the strongest religious feeling he ever evinced was a negative one, consisting in intense dislike for the Romish Church." He was a man of "high moral worth and refined literary tastes," and in so far as he had any profession, it was that of a scientific chemist. On his return from India, where he made his fortune, he had accepted the post of head lecturer on chemistry in the Apothecaries' Hall, Dublin, in order to have something to do. He seems to have had a worse horror of the vulgarity of the Catholic religion than even had his wife, owing to "the circumstances of his birth and position in society." Fortunately for him, he came into relation with a dignified gentlemanly Catholic priest, Dr Armstrong, and, strange to say, he also turned completely to faith, and was received before he died, "and spent the remainder of his life, almost a year, in the fervent practice of every virtue he could practise on his bed of sickness." One day he suddenly asked Catherine why she had let Mrs Callahan die without making some effort to instruct her; "for you know," said he, "that she was not even baptised." And his adopted daughter then told him what had occurred.

"On the 11th of November 1822, William Callahan, fortified by the last Sacraments, at peace with God and man, and consoled with the hope of a blessed eternity, fell asleep in the Lord. His will declared his adopted daughter, Catherine Callahan M'Aulay, his sole heiress. He left her absolute mistress of his wealth, without even expressing a wish as to how it should be disposed of." He told Dr Armstrong that she would do good with it. And so she did! Four years later some effort seems to have been made to contest the will, on the ground of insanity, but it was easy to disprove this, and in 1826 Miss M'Aulay had already bought the Baggot Street site, and all the world understood what she was going to do with her money. She sold the fine old house at Coolock, where she had been brought up, with the library, pictures, and as much of the furniture as she considered unsuitable for the institution she contemplated. The one luxury she kept was her carriage. It could be turned to use.

All this time Catherine had not the remotest idea of founding a religious institute. She had built, for charitable purposes, her house in Baggot

Street, amidst much opposition and even ridicule from the male members of her own family; previously, says her candid biographer, they had been satisfied with her determination to lead a single life, perhaps hoping that she would remain a wealthy and benevolent aunt to their children, but when they saw her money flowing out over " persons whom they could not consider as visitors," and she herself settling down into a big barrack, as they considered her new erection, then her own brother, and her sister's husband, both of them good Protestant gentlemen, who had always remained much attached to her, raised angry lamentations, and urged her to accept an eligible suitor, one Major W——, who had more than once urged himself on her acceptance and had not relinquished his hopes. How they scolded and implored is told with considerable vivacity. But Miss M'Aulay, who was now nearly forty years of age, knew her own mind, which at this time was bent on keeping up a Refuge in company with certain other ladies, and working hard among the Dublin poor with the comfortable aid of her own fortune. The strangest part of the whole story is the way in which she was led, step by step, without warning or intention, into the career which, in ten years, almost the remainder of her comparatively short life, was to make her name known over the whole civilised world, and required to train women who, after her own death, went off to nurse our wounded soldiers in the Crimea. The last of that band, decorated by the Queen in the year of Diamond Jubilee, died since these pages were begun.

"The Institute continued to make rapid progress. In 1829 several of the ladies who assisted in the schools manifested a desire to reside entirely on the premises. The order and discipline observed, the stated times of prayer and silence, the responsibility which materially devolved on the Foundress and made others apply to her for direction, gave the Institute more the appearance of a convent than the pious projector had anticipated."

It was in this early time that Daniel O'Connell, with his wife and daughters, appeared on the scene; he had been for some time acquainted with Miss M'Aulay, and her work had his warmest sympathies. There was in O'Connell's character a strong vein of piety which was not at all understood by the English Liberals amidst whom his parliamentary life was cast, but which is revealed in his private diary. In his journeys through Ireland he nearly always visited the convents, when addresses were read by the pupils, to which he replied in his style of ornate magnificence; and on one occasion he said to the girls grouped round the youthful speaker: "Are you born for no better lot than slavery? No; you *shall* be free. Your country shall yet be a nation; you shall not become the mothers of slaves!" In Baggot Street he was a well-known figure. In 1827, Miss M'Aulay had begun the custom of entertaining all the poor children of the neighbourhood at Christmas. O'Connell came to preside. "He had a pleasant word for every one of them, and their lean, sickly faces soon reflected the happiness of his fine, good-humoured countenance." This

Christmas dinner remains almost universal in the Order of Mercy.

But it is now necessary to record certain trials which befell Miss M'Aulay in the beginning of her career, and to speak of them with peculiar reserve, as they relate to the action of the revered Archbishop Murray. It has been told in previous pages how Dr Murray had in past years laid, with the most supreme care and intelligence, the solid foundations of the Order of the Sisters of Charity in Ireland. He had chosen his helper in the youthful Mary Aikenhead; had sent her and Alicia Walsh to be trained at the Bar Convent in York, and had rallied round them, on their return in 1815, all the charitable assistance, all the prayers, all the best and most intelligent workers he could command. For them he had said masses innumerable; for them he had cherished and aided vocations — they were the dear children of his heart. He was already waxing old, and he had hewn this solid staff ready to his hand. He had trained these Sisters for the Arch-diocese and for Ireland, lending them out, as it were, to other Bishops—to Cork first, afterwards to Waterford and Galway—to render back increase of souls and devoted work to the Mother House in Dublin. It is evident that he could not at first look with eyes of certain favour on a diversion of the stream of fervour and charity from this regular channel. Catherine M'Aulay was independent of him through her fortune, which was very large for Ireland, and she was evidently one of those souls who possess an extraordinary power of immediate attraction on other souls. The very gates of Jericho fell down before her. The most unlikely old people made their submission on their deathbeds if Catherine were anywhere about. Children clung to her and insisted that, being orphaned of their mother, they would live with no one but their aunt; and to the dismay of her brother, his daughters flung themselves into her work. It was the same with young ladies on the outside. She was a sort of Pied Piper of Hamelin. They gathered to her, they foregathered with her; they went to live with her in the big new barrack; they left off their fine clothes and put on a plain dress; they said prayers with zealous exactitude at fixed hours; but they made no vows, and some of them finally became "holy wives and mothers." It is quite clear, from reading the account of those first years, that the Archbishop felt a flood of devotion rising round his feet, and that he hesitated how best to channel it, and irrigate the fields. "Several zealous persons having represented to him that the new Institute was being changed into a Convent, without being bound by any of the rules authorised by the Church, His Grace admitted the inconvenience of this, and said that the idea of a conventual establishment starting up of itself in this manner had never entered into his mind. Indeed, the position of the Institute was somewhat anomalous. It was not a convent, being bound by no rule or vow, nor could it, with propriety, be styled a secular house, for it had already its appointed hours of silence and recreation, of labour and rest, of prayer and study. Yet not one of those concerned ever thought of it becoming the cradle of a new religious congregation; but what founder ever saw at a glance the consequences of his work? . . . Just as little did Catherine anticipate the future, when she erected a house to shelter a few poor women."

We are further told that she had the greatest reverence for the Archbishop, and had for years been accustomed to rely on his guidance; and to have incurred his displeasure by any ill-advised step, or series of acts, even if wholly prompted by zeal and devotion, would have caused her the keenest pain; and she wrote to him, "offering to resign into his hands the house just completed, begging that he would be pleased to allow her the poorest apartment in it, and permission to labour in any capacity to carry out her good intentions." But Dr Murray contemplated no such drastic measure; he was simply anxious how to proceed; and he told her that "every good work was destined to be opposed and contradicted, and for trials she should be ever prepared." Just then an old friend of Miss M'Aulay's, Dr Blake, returned from Rome, and did his best to ease her mind. Visiting her one day, Dr Blake remarked that the Institute was now like its Divine Master—a sign to be contradicted. "But," added he, "it is high time to rescue you and your associates from the anomaly of your present position; you have endured it long enough." He then went to confer with the Archbishop, and after a consultation between them, it was decided that the Sisters of Mercy must appear definitely as religious or seculars; "and as they unanimously chose to become religious, it was also decided that their Institute should be entirely unconnected with any other, that it should be governed by its own rules and constitutions, and that the practices of monastic life as such, should, as soon as possible, be introduced among its members."

The next step was to get Miss M'Aulay and a few of her associates regularly trained and professed; and this was accomplished by the help of the Presentation nuns, who were established in Ireland in the previous century by the efforts of a well-known and indefatigable Irish lady—Nano Nagle. These nuns are bound to the education of the poor only; originally they visited the sick, but they are, by their constitution, a cloistered order. The Archbishop offered to invite some professed members of that order to Baggot Street, or to allow Miss M'Aulay and a few of her associates to make a novitiate in some Presentation Convent, and this latter was the course adopted. She, and her first companion, Miss Doyle, and a third, Miss Elizabeth Harley, went to the convent at St George's Hill, a spacious but dreary-looking building, situated in the most densely populated part of Dublin. It was erected in 1794, at a time when Catholic institutions did not dare show themselves in respectable localities. Here the three postulants were received at the gate by the Superioress and the community, and here they remained for a year and three months. Here they took their final vows, according to the Presentation form, with the proviso that the vow of

HISTORIC NUNS

obedience might include whatever the Church should subsequently approve for the Order of Mercy. They returned to Baggot Street on the 12th of December 1831, and from that day is dated the foundation of the order, though the institute had been in constant operation since 1827. Eight years later, Catherine M'Aulay revisited St George's Hill; and in a letter dated in November 1839, she says, " the affectionate nuns were delighted to see us. I essayed to embrace the old rush chair on which I used to sit, but I kissed a grand new one in mistake; however, I took back the kiss, as 'ducky Mary Grail' (one of the orphan children) would say, and bestowed it on the right chair."

When the three newly-professed nuns got to Baggot Street in 1831 they found the Sisters whom they had left, and several others who had flocked in during their absence, in the chapel awaiting their arrival, with Dr Blake, their faithful friend. A *Te Deum* was sung, and then he addressed a few impressive words to the assemblage. The house was already peopled with children, and with the poor. Mother M'Aulay, as she was now called, found her old work well kept together and ready to her hand; and a month later seven of the ladies who had conducted the establishment during her year of absence, were clothed with the habit of the new order, the Archbishop presiding; thus Dr Murray had laid his strong hand upon the zealous spirits who were, in the beginning, like fiery steeds ready to spring, as later experience showed, to the ends of the earth. Not one grain of that splendid energy was wasted in future years. Heat veritably became a mode of motion.

The first work undertaken in Baggot Street seems to have been the housing of distressed women of good character, and Mrs M'Aulay was quite inflexible on this qualification. But she sometimes stretched a point as regards a night's lodging; keeping the doubtful applicant away from the inmates. One night, at a late hour (it was in 1829), the few ladies residing at the House were startled by a violent ringing at the bell. When the door was opened, a young girl, half stupefied with cold and fatigue, implored shelter for the night, saying she had travelled a long way on foot, and had no friends in Dublin. She looked so wild and untidy, that the Foundress conceived unfavourable suspicions of her; but, as there could be no doubt about her distress, a comfortable meal was prepared for her, and she was allowed to remain till morning. The poor creature, after having eaten a little, told her name and story. She had quarrelled with a harsh stepmother, and, in the excitement of the moment, had run away, she knew not whither, from her father's home. Regretting her imprudence when it was too late to return, she walked on to Dublin, hoping to get admission into some house of refuge; and, having applied to one, she was told she had not the slightest chance for many days, as the committee received information only at stated times. The woman who gave her this unwelcome information, moved by the poor girl's tears, directed her to Baggot Street. Next morning one of the ladies recognised the wanderer as the daughter of an attorney who practised in a small town not many miles from Dublin, and who had lately, to the great annoyance of his grown-up children, contracted a second marriage. She was kept at Baggot Street till provided with a situation as governess in a respectable family; but, happily, her father soon forgave her, and took her home.

"For many months after the opening of the House, its inmates, and the strangers who applied for work or admission, met daily in a large hall for instruction and prayer. Mother M'Aulay often spoke of the honesty of these poor visitors. As long as she kept what she pleasantly called 'open house,' there was never anything stolen, except an old chair on which she used to sit when instructing them, and which was probably abstracted as a relic by some devotee who regarded the usual occupant as a saint. However, as the number to be instructed increased, she separated the inmates entirely from the externals, to guard against the danger of admitting persons of exceptionable character among the young women of the House of Mercy, that being exclusively for such as bore untarnished reputations."

The second object of the Order of Mercy is the visitation of the sick, and also of prisons and hospitals. While living in the world, Mother M'Aulay had been used to drive round to the different hospitals in her carriage, asking to be allowed to instruct and console the sick. When she presented herself in the garb of a Sister of Mercy, the governors and officials recognised their old friend. It was long after her own death that the great hospital of the Mater

Misericordiæ housed two thousand patients under the exclusive care of the Sisterhood.

Another main object, and, indeed, the primary end of the Order of Mercy, was the instructing of the ignorant; the getting real thought and real principle into the minds of children and empty-headed adults. To this end Mother M'Aulay spared no pains in training the young Sisters for their duties. Besides a thorough English education, which she considered indispensable, she made the Sisters keep up music, for the Church; painting, useful in many ways; and foreign languages, so necessary for the Sisters who visited the prisons and hospitals of seaport towns. The chapter about the schools is very interesting, and full of detail. It refers to the mixed National Board of Education, on which Dr Murray and Dr Whately sat side by side, and records that the experiment of mixed education proved a failure in Ireland. It also describes how she laboured for the middle classes. "In looking on the numerous conventual establishments in Ireland, the keen penetration of the Foundress saw that they were all too exclusive. There were Ursuline Schools for the rich, and Presentation Schools for the poor, but no provision was made for the middle classes. This was also the case with male institutions. There were Jesuits for the upper classes, and Christian Schools for the lower, while boys of a middle grade, who could not afford to go to the first, and whom an honest pride would prevent from going to the second, were unprovided with religious teachers." And she opened day schools for the middle classes in Cork, Carlow, Galway, and other places. "Perhaps no one person ever did so much for the cause of education in the lower and middle classes as did Mother M'Aulay; but then, she seemed an educationalist by nature, born, not made, as was said of the poets of old. But no one could fail to become an excellent teacher, however dull her natural intellect might be, who constantly laboured and prayed so earnestly to become one. She did not ask Divine Providence to work miracles for her; she put her own hand to the work; she applied to it as if the salvation of the whole world depended on her exertions, and then calmly left the issue to Him. And He blessed her labour beyond her own most sanguine expectations. She lived to see her order conferring a Christian education on thousands of the poor; and to-day, if she looks down from heaven on her scattered children, she will find their pupils amount to nearly 200,000—including those of industrial, infant, and literary schools — scattered through the British Islands, North and South America, Australia, New Zealand."

This was written in 1866, thirty-two years ago.

It must be recorded of the early years of the Order of Mercy that several deaths occurred at Baggot Street among the younger Sisters; whether in that first ardour the zeal of the religious life outran discretion, or whether it happened that the seeds of consumption existed in several of the postulants, it were now useless to inquire. The Foundress suffered keenly, and especially at the death of her beloved young niece, Mary Teresa

M'Aulay, but these deaths, far from frightening the others, inside and outside the House, seemed only to provoke an accession of self-devotion. Although they were actively engaged, like the Sisters of Charity, in nursing the cholera patients of 1832, none died of the pestilence, and after the first beginning no unusual mortality occurred. In 1838 there were more than a hundred Sisters of Mercy, but every new foundation was a fresh centre of attraction, and their numbers soon increased by leaps and bounds.

The Rule and Constitution of the Institute was not formally completed till 1834, nor approved by authority till the following year. The basis of the Rule was that of St Augustine, of which the Presentation Rule is but another form. But it required modification and adaptation to modern circumstances. "Taken as a whole, it may be regarded as a faithful exponent of Mother M'Aulay's views on religious perfection, and in writing it she unconsciously drew her own portrait. It is concise, but nothing essential is omitted. Ardent charity, profound humility, and tender piety pervade every section." Before this essential work was completed she lost the help and direction of her good friend, Dr Blake—he who had persuaded the Archbishop to revise his first opinion of the undertaking in Baggot Street, and was to her a wall of defence. Dr Blake was made Bishop of Dromore, and removed to his new residence.

But the time was approaching when the young order was to enter on spheres of such extended usefulness that all opposition fell before accomplished facts. Nevertheless, the very first outside start was not a happy one. One of the curates at Kingstown, on Dublin Bay, begged hard that Catherine M'Aulay would establish a school there. The pastor, who was old and delicate, for a long time refused to assist, except by his patronage, but he at last offered "to do something." The curate begged her to make a start, and she purchased a house and sent a few Sisters, who began with a school of 300 children. The zealous curate, Mr Walsh,* afterwards became Archbishop of Halifax, Nova Scotia. Many were the troubles endured by the Sisters at Kingstown, but these were finally compensated by the erection of a convent and schools in the neighbouring parish of Booterstown. The ground belonged to the Honourable Sidney Herbert, and he had given it through the medium of Mrs Verschoyle, a pious friend of his, and he had also taken upon himself a large share of the expense of the erections. This is the Convent of St Ann, which was opened in 1838.

The first branch of the Institute outside the Archdiocese was that of Tullamore. Dr Cantwell, the Bishop of Meath, asked for Sisters, and Miss Pentony, a wealthy charitable lady, bequeathed her house and an annuity to establish Sisters of Mercy in her native town. They were received with the greatest delight by the people, and the Vicar-General of Meath went to Dublin to escort the

* Archbishop Walsh appears to have been translated to Toronto, where he lately died.

Sisters to their new home. Mother M'Aulay herself went with them, and stayed a month; two new postulants joined her there. The house was so small and awkward, that the Foundress, "whose sight was beginning to grow dim," was several times in danger of falling over the uneven steps in the passage. But two years later she was able to write that the new convent and schools at Tullamore were "a grand tribute to religion, and a very handsome sight from the canal boat; indeed, they are quite an ornament to the town. . . . They will last for centuries."

After Tullamore came Carlow Convent, and after that Charleville; and later the foundation at Cork. This latter was of course extremely important; and here a spacious and well-adapted house, fully furnished in conventual style, was presented to the Sisters, with a gift of £2000, by Miss Barbara Gould. As I have spoken at some length of the foundation made by the Sisters of Charity at "Cork Castle," I will not repeat a similar experience in the same city, only saying that the first house, which, though convenient, had a very small garden, and was situated in a gloomy locality near one of the quays, was in a few years replaced by the magnificent Gothic convent now known as St Marie's of the Isle, which stands on an islet between two branches of the river Lee, on the site of an ancient Dominican Abbey which bore the same name before the Reformation. At St Marie's, 1200 children receive gratuitous education; there is also here a Mercy Hospital, and an industrial school where some hundreds of girls earn their livelihood.

It is time to leave Ireland and see what impression Catherine M'Aulay was making upon us in England. It is a very curious story, and it begins with an English Catholic prelate, Dr Griffiths, Vicar-Apostolic of the London district. He was the son of a carpenter, and was born in 1791 of a mixed marriage, his mother only being Catholic. His father sent him to a Protestant school, where his schoolfellows nicknamed him the bishop. But his father died, and his mother sent him to St Edmund's College in his fourteenth year, where he studied for the priesthood, having always manifested an ardent affection for his mother's faith. This man of the people had an open mind and heart, and after his ordination in 1814, he became successively President of St Edmund's (while still under thirty years of age), and some years later coadjutor to Bishop Bramstone, whom he succeeded in 1836. It was said by somebody that "he had the madness" to open a correspondence with Mrs M'Aulay, with the view of getting her nuns across the Channel to help his poor; and as she listened to his request, he sent over two English ladies to be trained in the convent at Cork; one of these was Miss Agnew, authoress of "Geraldine," a religious novel which had an extraordinary vogue some seventy years ago. The first and second volumes of this work were published before the authoress became a Sister of Mercy—the third after. The other was Miss Taylor. Elizabeth Constantia Agnew was niece to Sir Andrew Agnew, a celebrated antiquarian, and Member of Parliament for Wigtownshire. She was in middle life when she went to Cork, having been born in 1798, and a highly accomplished woman of the world; she lived into her eighty-fourth year. About Miss Taylor there was nothing brilliant; she was about thirty in 1838, and both ladies had previously been working under Father Butler in the district of Bermondsey, in the companionship of Lady Barbara Eyre (a daughter of Lord Newburgh), and several others, and they had adopted a plain black dress, and kept school in a building called the old Chapel House, where they were very uncomfortable, as it was little better than a ruin. Some of these zealous ladies wished for a more contemplative life and some for a more active one. Their plans were quite inchoate, just as Catherine M'Aulay's plans had originally been in Baggot Street; but their ideas and desires were being slowly and divinely moulded. Money seems not to have been lacking from the first, as a piece of land had been bought and plans for a convent procured from Augustus Pugin, the great architect of French extraction, who built so many beautiful churches, and is popularly supposed to have had a good deal to do with Sir Charles Barry's drawings for the Houses of Parliament. This house at Bermondsey went up rapidly under his direction, and was the first monastic structure erected in London since the Reformation.

"Postage was slow at this period, and there was little or no steam communication between England and Ireland, so that good enterprises had time to mature in one country before their fame reached the other. Yet the new order was known very early in England. A priest on the London mission had sent Mother Catherine the first English convert received in Baggot Street in 1830. Bishop Griffiths and Father Butler were so well pleased with its scope and spirit that they selected it as the order best adapted for the sanctification of the ladies under their direction, and the benefit of the poor."—*The Annals of the Order.*

So two of these ladies were selected, and sent across the sea that they might be trained and professed, and form a nucleus for the new English convent, and they were met at Cork on the 4th of April 1838, by the Bishop and two priests—Father Mathew himself, and Father Delany—and were greeted with a warmth for which, says the writer of "The Annals," "they were quite unprepared." Indeed, the two middle-aged English ladies, sedate and undemonstrative as they usually were, were affected to tears by the cordiality of the welcome on all sides. "Being converts, and no longer young, they were at first treated with a degree of deference uncommon in the strict novitiate of which they formed—in conventual parlance—the infant band. Their conduct, however, gave unlimited satisfaction, and in July they were allowed to enter on the ten days' retreat that precedes reception, having previously made a distinct retreat of three weeks." After the profession, Mrs M'Aulay took them to Tullamore, and with them the young Mother, Clare Moore, who was barely five-and-twenty, but whom the Foundress had picked out for the Superiorship of the English convent; she had joined Mother Catherine at sixteen, being professed three years later, and her extreme timidity was the most remarkable of her external qualities! Yet she had been sent to Cork in 1837 to found the convent there, and was carried off to London full of "dread and dislike of the troublesome charge." She was so shy that she clung at first to Mrs M'Aulay, and would not see visitors without her; but Dr Griffiths, who had seen her, had "mentally selected her as the person to introduce the order into England, and this, no doubt, had something to do with the choosing of the Cork house for the novitiate of the English Sisters."

This timid girl made a splendid nun, and from that time to her death, thirty-seven years later, was never released from the Superiorship.

On Monday, November 18th, 1840, the little group of travelling nuns left Ireland for Liverpool, under the guidance of the Foundress, whose travelling title was "Friend Catherine." They had a very bad passage, and their first mishap was to lose the early train. Forty years later, the one survivor of the little group wrote: "I was glad of the delay, and said it was permitted for my good, for I was sick and cold, and there was a fine fire in the waiting-room"; but the others were too anxious to reach London by daylight to feel the same. Nearly all were new to travel by railway. In England it was only ten years since the launching of that first fatal train between Liverpool and Manchester which cost Mr Huskisson his life; and in Ireland the Annals of the two orders of travelling nuns show that they constantly went from town to town in canal boats! When the tired party reached London it was past eleven, and near midnight when they reached the house of Father Butler, the priest of the Bermondsey district. He himself was lying on what was supposed to be his deathbed; he had been overworking in his anxiety to have everything ready for the nuns, and had burst a blood-vessel. His sister, who was nursing him, gave the weary nuns some supper, and they then went over to the unfinished convent, where there was one furnished room into which they packed as best they could. Both in the Life and in the Annals, a very unflattering picture is given of the Bermondsey Convent. It was the time of the Pugin craze, when, as a friend once remarked to the compiler of this story, "even the salt cellars were Gothic." Mrs M'Aulay had been reared in quite other traditions; the old Irish chapels were square, as may be seen in country districts to this day, and the floors often of beaten earth, and when the congregations overflowed, they knelt outside on the road—a sight which no one who had seen it could ever forget; and when a new church was achieved, it was made as roomy as possible, like St Teresa's in Clarendon Street. And the building in Bermondsey was unfinished, and she wrote that it "was not likely to be dry for three years." This melancholy state of things in November was one of the causes of the undermining of Catherine M'Aulay's health, though she survived for two years. Neither was there air and light. "Mr Pugin was determined we should not look out of the windows, they are up to the ceiling. We could not touch the glass without standing on a chair. We have one good room finished, with brown walls and a long table. There is too much room in some places, and too little in others. The noviceship is very small, the kitchen fit for a castle. It is nearly the best room in the house." . . . "The heart of the Foundress sank as she walked through the bleak corridors of the unfinished mansion. The nuns were chilled through and through whenever they attempted to move from the corner they inhabited. The poor Mother grieved, knowing how little they could do if health failed them." Nevertheless, nobody was really deterred, and six ladies, who had been doing duty in the old Chapel House, entered a week after the arrival of the colony—the principal among them being Lady Barbara Eyre, who possessed fortune and an ardent desire to forward the foundation. Bishop Griffiths came on the day after the arrival from Ireland, and insisted on giving Mrs M'Aulay a fifty-pound note. In vain she assured him they were provided with all to which they had been accustomed. The reception of Lady Barbara Eyre was a splendid function, as she seems for the last time to have worn a court-dress and feathers! She was simple enough in herself, good soul, and she and her family only desired to bring all the social prestige they could to the undertaking. But Mrs M'Aulay would never again allow any material to be used in the dresses of the postulants which could not afterwards be devoted to the service of the sanctuary.

Catherine M'Auley got back to Dublin in January, quite broken in health from the privations and fatigues of her recent mission. "The sacrifice of her life seems to have been the great cross destined to consolidate her Institute in England. Her remaining twenty-two months of life were months of martyrdom." The room she occupied while in Bermondsey is now a sacristy opening on the new chapel. In this same room Mother Clare died after a long life of labour. The frightened young Superior founded one branch convent after another; and it was she who headed the band of nuns who went to nurse our soldiers in the Crimean War. But at the date at which we arrived, she found herself immediately plunged into severe trouble at home. Typhus broke out among the poor population down by the river, and three of the Sisters caught it from a stricken family. Two of them died; one was Mary O'Connor, in religion called Sister Ursula; she was young, and had already been working at the old Chapel House since 1838. The other was a middle-aged nun of forty, who had lived much in religious houses on the Continent, but had never bound herself to any order, until she heard of the Sisters of Mercy. She was particularly fond of teaching children—she died four or five days after Mary O'Connor; her family name is not given. The third Sister recovered after a struggle. The widow and her eight children, whom the three had been nursing, all recovered. To realise the dangers to which the nuns were exposed, we must recall to mind the nursing trials of sixty years ago, before the days of fresh air and antiseptics. Poor young Mother Clare did not fall ill, but she was completely prostrated for the moment, and she wrote to a correspondent in Carlow: "Picture us to yourself going to the vault with one dear Sister on Wednesday, and another the following Saturday. . . . My heart is gone"; and the recipient copying out the passage, probably for Mrs M'Aulay, adds: "You would not know her handwriting." The greatest sympathy was shown the Bermondsey nuns; strangers and Protestants called and offered their services, and an anonymous poet rang the bell and offered some original lines to the portress. His name never transpired, but here are two of the verses:

> "Death entered the convent—two victims were fated;
> They listened, they sank, ere they laid down to die.
> Round their beds the sad Sisterhood kneeling awaited
> The last look, the last word, the last long-drawn sigh.
> King of terrors! thy summons were sudden and fearful:
> It startled us, thrilled us, and filled us with dread.
> Our souls are still dark, our eyes are still tearful:
> Five suns—a brief space—and two spirits are fled."

These two deaths were followed by the almost immediate entrance of four more postulants!

Then followed a winter of exceptional severity. From Ireland Mrs M'Aulay wrote: "I never saw such frost"; and the young Mother at Bermondsey wrote that the winter in London was more severe than any for a century; but this was a mistake, though what sailors call the white swan—a cloud of snow floating in the air—had been seen near

Winchester. Four years before, in 1837, the Thames was frozen as hard and smooth as a deal board; and the compiler of this story well remembers begging hard to be allowed to walk about twenty feet from the Westminster bank, holding on to a man-servant. That was the winter when an ox was roasted whole upon the ice; and this may be a fit place to mention that the Puginesque Convent, which "looked like a prison," was (and is) so near the Thames, that the periodical spring tides do not always spare it; and, some years later, "the water was two feet deep in the kitchen and other apartments of the lowest storey, and fish were caught in the refectory. Milk was brought by a man on horseback, and, while he was delivering his freight, the animal, getting tired of disporting himself in the water, walked into the convent, to the great discomfiture of the portress, and the amusement of the rest."

The account of Bermondsey Convent must draw to a close: it is but a mere page of the whole story; but to us in England it is a particularly interesting page, and to me it is especially associated with my friend Agnes Procter, who here began her novitiate, but was transferred to Chelsea, because of the unhealthy situation of the older house. At Chelsea I was present at her profession, sitting in a gallery of the chapel with her sister Adelaide.

From "dear old Bermondsey," as its children fondly consider it, in spite of frost, flood, and fever, were planted all those houses which now girdle London with a belt of mercy. The first offshoot was the noble convent in Blandford Square; being on the

Middlesex side of the river, it was the first in London proper. It was planned in 1842, and the Sisters were temporarily lodged in Queen's Square, Bloomsbury, while the buildings farther west were slowly rising. It was not till December 15, 1849, that Dr Wiseman wrote to the Superior that "at length" he had heard that the charge was likely to be undertaken, and that, therefore, he would allow and favour her efforts to procure the necessary funds, and wished her all success. While in Queen Square the Sisters had been chiefly occupied in attending daily six or seven Catholic poor schools, and visiting the sick poor of the neighbourhood. Round the corner, in Great Ormond Street, was established the hospital called St Elizabeth and St John of Jerusalem, entirely under charge of the Sisters of Mercy. It has lately been removed to St John's Wood. At Blandford Square, the convent occupies the whole of the western side, and carries on a group of splendid charities. Some years ago, the number of destitute young women of good character who had been admitted to the dormitories, and provided with situations, amounted to 4000. The nuns visited daily at the Marylebone Workhouse Infirmary for years, and when this was moved into better air at Notting Hill, the Sisters were still summoned by a post-card. In 1869, Dr Manning, then Archbishop, summoned a great meeting of the reverend Mothers and their assistants of the Archdiocese of Westminster, at the Convent of Blandford Square; but want of sufficient sleeping accommodation precluded the full carrying out of the plan. However, exclusive of the Sisters of Mercy, there were eighty-one religious present. During meals the Sisters of Mercy waited on their guests, taking their own meals afterwards. Dr Manning gave a retreat of three days, and eighteen other orders were represented; many, if not all, having several houses in different parts of the Archdiocese. Indeed, I cannot keep track of the numbers organised, living and working, in any one particular year. They steadily increase, so that what was true of 1870 is outstepped in 1880, 1890, and 1898. Of course, an accurate record is in each case obtainable, if wanted.

Before returning to the Foundress, whose remaining time on earth was a very short span, it seems simpler to follow the career of Mother Clare, at least as far as the epoch of the Crimean War. It was that timid young nun of 1840, who clung to the skirts of Mother M'Aulay, and would not at first face strangers without her support, who in 1856 headed the little troop whom Bishop Grant sent off to look after the sick and wounded soldiers of their own faith. Bishop Grant had travelled with his father's regiment when a boy. Sergeant Grant and his wife were Catholics from the north of Ireland. Bermondsey Convent was in his diocese, and the only one which carried on the visitation of the sick, and thither he came on the 13th of October 1854, and told Mother Clare that she must send out nuns to the Crimea. She knew nothing whatever about war and wounded soldiers, and thought the Bishop was jesting; but when he explained the horrors of the Eastern hospitals, she immediately offered to go herself. At first he thought it impossible to spare her from London, but two days later he wrote to her to pick out four other nuns, and "start for Turkey to-morrow." And start they did on the 17th. An elderly friend, Bishop Morris (a bishop *in partibus*), came to the convent, with his eyes full of tears, and asked, "Who is to take care of you from here to Turkey?" "Our angel guardians," was the reply. He could do nothing for the pilgrims, but he went every week to Bermondsey during their absence to look after those who were left behind. To Paris the five set off, knowing probably as little of our so familiar tidal train as we ourselves should know of a journey by balloon. When they reached Paris, the Hotel Meurice, to which they had been directed, had not a vacant room, and Mr Goldsmid, to whom the Bishop had given them a letter of introduction, had gone to bed, and the porter refused to knock him up. But he took them to the Hotel Clarendon, and there they met with a kind reception; and, on their return from church in the early morning, they found Mr Goldsmid waiting to see them. Miss Nightingale was in Paris, and called on them with a grateful welcome; they spent a week in the French metropolis, and every possible courtesy was shown to them in the great hospitals. They bought cases of surgical instruments and other stores; and the French nuns at St Roch taught them as much as they could in the time; the Bishop wrote to them every day, and so did the flock in Bermondsey, to whom Mother Clare replied with astonishing pluck, and told them that the Government had consented to employ them, and to recognise them as nuns; she added: "Now, pray that we may do everything very well and give great satisfaction. Try to keep all at Bermondsey well and happy—Sisters, children, and all. I have you all within my heart, and say an *Ave* for you all three times a day, besides the accustomed devotions."

They finally traversed the Mediterranean in a violent storm, and reached Constantinople on the 4th of November, thousands of spectators coming to see them land and climb up the steep hill from the landing-place to the barracks. There the Sisters were put into a large room, which was absolutely unfurnished, except for one old chair, which, being without a back, served also for a table. The windows were broken, and there was no fire. An energetic soldier set to work to make some tea; alas, it was made in a can, and was of the weakest description. But the nuns ever after regarded him most gratefully.

Then Mother Clare fell to work. The other four spent their time dressing wounds, and two of them caught the hospital fever, and nearly died. But they pulled through, and refused to be sent home. Mother Clare was forced to remain daily for hours serving out stores to the medical officers and nurses. Some items of the daily average may be gathered from the official report: "25 gallons arrowroot, 15 gallons chicken broth, 40 gallons arrowroot, 240 quarts barley-water, 100 bottles port wine,

mixed in the proportionate quantity of arrowroot."
No nurse was allowed in this department. She had
to receive, prepare, and give out, aided by a contingent of Greeks, Italians, Turks, French, and
soldiers employed as orderlies, whom the nurses
called Alderneys! This motley throng was ruled
by the nun so efficiently that, in the graver cases,
if anything went wrong, it sufficed to uplift a finger.
"The Greeks and Turks obeyed her as exactly as if
they understood every word she uttered."

Many more Sisters went out, collected from
convents of the order in England and Ireland;
Liverpool, Dublin, Chelsea, Kinsale, Charleville,
Carlow, and Cork contributed their quota. But
the Bermondsey Sisters went out as a private
charity a month before the great excitement about
the Crimean miseries arose. The father of the
present Duke of Norfolk defrayed the expense of
the expedition; the Sisters risked their lives
(Mother Clare nearly died). And when, at the
end of the war, the Guards returned in the same
ship with a last detachment, the commanding
officer asked them to share the triumph of the
landing by walking at the head of the regiment
from the ship to the neighbouring barracks. "On
the way, the people who had assembled to cheer
the soldiers began to groan at the religious, where-
upon one of the men became so exasperated that
he sprang from the ranks and called upon his
comrades to defend the ladies who had stood so
faithfully by their dying brethren-in-arms. The
regiment to a man placed themselves in a threaten-

ing attitude, with their rifles levelled at the crowd—a serious position, as all were supplied with ball cartridges. The commander stepped between the regiment and the people, and in a few well-chosen words explained the relation in which the nuns stood to them, the labours, fatigues, and indescribable sufferings they had endured for love of humanity. The hooting then turned to cheering, and the nuns, as they marched on, became the unwilling objects of an ovation. From that day Sisters of Mercy can walk through London, not only unmolested, but respected."

One such Sister survived until the Diamond Jubilee of last year, and was decorated by the Queen, having been summoned from her retirement for the purpose. I believe she has since passed away.

And now the temptation is great to carry the reader again across the sea, to the splendid convents and schools in Australia—to Melbourne and Geelong—and tell how a long-lost nephew of the Foundress turned up, and placed his daughter, Jessie M'Aulay, at school with the nuns. And again across the sea to New Zealand, whither a band of nuns went from the Carlow Convent in 1849, being fetched by Bishop Pompalier, who had himself "had many a narrow escape from the Maori stomach." The Mother Superior of Carlow, by name Cecilia Maher, offered herself privately to him, though it was thought by all the community "a fearful mission." And "several others, urged by a similar inspiration, said, one unknown to the other, 'Here I am, send me.'" Dublin had recently sent Sisters to Australia and America, and could not help; so Carlow, in spite of "opposition from within and without," had to do the deed. Mother Cecilia was just fifty years of age. Her decision cost "much crying." She worked as Superior at Auckland until she was sixty-nine; then she had three years' rest as one of the community; but at seventy-two she was obliged to resume the burden. She worked on, "much bowed," until her eightieth year, and died in November 1878, in the summer weather of the Antipodes, her bier in the church being covered with "lilies and roses." A whole book might be written on Mother Cecilia, and how the natives whom she helped and taught refrained from "eating any member of community," or those of the five convents she founded. But though she was originally received by the Foundress (when nearly forty years of age), her work was done after Mrs M'Aulay's death, and to her it is necessary to return. Indeed, Catherine M'Aulay's own achievements must be divided mentally into two sections: the story of the eighteen foundations she made while on earth, and those which she virtually created after she had passed beyond sight; and *these* would lead us all over the world, and we should get tangled with so much travelling.

The two important foundations which received the last cares of the beloved Foundress were those of Liverpool and Birmingham. From the latter place she came home to die.

The first candidate for Liverpool was the youngest daughter of a Liverpool merchant. She was born in 1819, and was a clever, bright girl of twenty-two when, with the full consent of her parents, she gave herself to the work of a Sister of Mercy. Two of her brothers and an uncle were in the priesthood. Jane Frances, "Fanny" Gibson is one of the most attractive figures of the many who cross the pages of the Annals. She was trained at Baggot Street, at the same time with Mary Consitt, who came of a naval family. The "twin sisters in religion" worked together for forty years, and their deaths were not far apart; Fanny (Mother M. Lignori) died first, and within six months Mary Consitt (Sister Aloysius) failed. The first had been Superior for years; the latter shrank from responsibility, and worked ceaselessly among the poorest of Liverpool, and her death made an extraordinary impression on the town. "The poor came out of their dens and alleys in hundreds to gaze on the calm sweet features of their devoted friend; the highways and byways were cleared of the blind, the halt, the maimed; and many homes of the great ones of the earth were emptied to form the crowds that besieged the convent. Flowers were brought in abundance, and none departed without a little blossom sanctified by contact with the precious dead. Such weeping and wailing!. Poor creatures cried out that they had lost their mother, and one evidently spoke the sentiments of many when she said she wanted to die and be laid beside the good Sister. The plain deal coffin bore the inscription, 'Pray for the soul of Sister Mary Aloysius Consitt. Died April 28, 1882, aged 65 years.'"

We now come to the last months of Catherine M'Aulay's earthly life, which were as full of work as any preceding ones. In 1841, Dr Wiseman, who had so long been Rector of the English College in Rome, had been appointed coadjutor to Bishop Walsh in Birmingham, and President of the neighbouring College of Oscott. His sermons and his powerful personality had roused the Catholics of the Midlands to a fuller life, and to "an eager desire for a religious community on the part of the two bishops, the priests, and the people. A munificent gentleman, John Hardman, took upon himself the whole expense of building and furnishing a convent, and John, sixteenth Earl of Shrewsbury, gave £2000 towards the foundation fund. The Order of Mercy was selected as that most suitable to the spiritual and corporal wants of the place; and Juliana, daughter of Mr Hardman, with Miss Anne Wood, Miss Lucy Bond, and Miss Elizabeth Edwards, having offered themselves to Bishop Walsh for the community of religious, at once active and contemplative, which he designed to establish, were escorted to Dublin by Dr Wareing to make their novitiate under the holy Foundress herself in April 1840." Two more followed, and Mrs M'Aulay says that the English Sisters were most interesting, and that it seemed "extraordinary to find no vacant seat in the refectory after all the dear Sisters we have parted from in life and death." Indeed, Baggot Street had been sending its trained nuns to the right and the left and far across the sea, so that sometimes "the great barrack," which Miss M'Aulay had been censured for building, seemed quite empty to those who remained.

Dr Wiseman paid several visits to Dublin in 1840-41. He was anxious that the aged Bishop Walsh should come from Birmingham for the profession of the English Sisters in August (1840), but he and his coadjutor were summoned to London on law business. Archbishop Murray would have delayed their profession but for the alarming illness of Mr Hardman, who longed to see his daughter Juliana before his death. He actually did survive till 1844, but the fear sufficed to prevent delay, and the English Sisters were received by Archbishop Murray himself. He himself was quite old, and Mrs M'Aulay says: "He looks so heavenly and venerable that the English Sisters will never forget him. The effect will be most valuable to them, and we esteem it so great a favour to get him that we would not make any difficulty." And the transcriber in the Annals (probably a survivor of the band) adds: "One does not often see a countenance so eloquent of every virtue, so well adapted to confirm in the beholder the reverence a high and sacred office naturally inspires, as was that of Archbishop Murray; and even that accidental circumstance the Foundress turns to account."

Meanwhile, the "Pugin Convent," built to receive them, was rapidly rising, and it seems to have been a more cheerful edifice than that of Bermondsey; for Mrs M'Aulay gets over her prejudice against severe Gothic architecture, and says: "Their new convent is a beautiful Pugin structure. It could not be too nice for those whom God has destined to be its first occupants."

To the profession in Dublin came several distinguished persons from England; among them Dr Pusey and his daughters! And on the final departure for Birmingham, Mother Catherine went over with the English Sisters and remained with them a month. They reached Birmingham on the 21st of August 1841. We are told that "Her health caused much anxiety to those who knew something of her sufferings, but as she was ever calm, joyous, and hopeful, the Sisters did not fully realise her critical condition." And in another place she herself records that if she remained in a room with the window open she coughed all night, "and so I disturb the poor Sisters who are near me. When I return to Baggot Street, I expect to be confined to a close room, as the least blast makes me very troublesome for days together." She did leave Birmingham on the 23rd of September, having comforted old Mr Hardman, and placed his daughter Juliana as Superior in the new convent. After Mr Hardman's death in 1844, his widow lived as a boarder in the Convent for twenty-six years.

In 1881 this house was the only one which retained the Superior appointed by Mrs M'Aulay on its first establishment. Mother Juliana was still alive, and "had nobly done the work entrusted to her, and borne in obedience and resignation the burden of superiority which the holy Mother had found it so difficult to make her assume." For the young nuns upon whom Mrs M'Aulay laid her discerning hand were usually terrified at being obliged to govern others, and manage all the complicated business involved by carrying on what is really a house as much as any other house, and often containing more than a hundred people of all ages and conditions. The unknown writer of the Annals says (in 1881): "Truly when the holy Foundress looked upon Birmingham and loved it, she must have blessed it with effusion of heart. She saw it in the golden glow of a beautiful autumn, and bade it *good-bye* with a blessing, in September, her favourite month. And there is now only Mother Juliana who remembers that sad but hopeful parting; the rest have gone to their eternal home. What a beautiful remembrance for this aged religious, whose face is already turned towards Jerusalem! Her days must be serenely happy, whether life be for her all retrospect or partly prospect; the heavenly countenance of the holy Mother is in the past as well as before her, and her beloved child of early days may gaze hopefully, wistfully on the near future or the sweet past."

Mrs M'Aulay crossed St George's Channel by way of Liverpool, taking with her the young novice, Fanny Gibson, who there met her mother, and they visited a large gloomy-looking house on Mount Vernon, which was being fitted up by the very Rev. Dr Youens for a temporary convent. The day was wet and cold, and Mrs M'Aulay, who did not much consider her own health, got damp; the voyage to Ireland was stormy, and when she reached Kingston the Sisters saw a grievous change in her appearance. But on the morning of the next day she writes off to Mother

Frances, who was, I think, at Cork, full of interest about the projected foundation at Liverpool, describing how she had dined with Dr Youens, and how a very nice person, a Miss Consitt, had been sent by him to Baggot Street during her absence. And she seems to have expressed a keen interest about America, the Bishop of Newfoundland having applied for nuns. At that time the Irish people knew little or nothing about the western world. Persons of good abilities and information in other respects imagined it "a vast prairie in which Indians and buffaloes wrestled for dominion." But Catherine M'Aulay would herself have taken over a band of her nuns had health remained. Indeed, in October 1841 she had one of those rallies so frequent in lung disease, and on the 8th she wrote to Dr Burke of Westport: "Many thanks dear Rev. Father, for the kind concern you express about my health. I am really quite a fine lady, doing nothing but looking on, *keeping up the little remnant for foundations*, and, above all, for Westport." And she writes to Galway, where she had been the previous year, and where a Miss Joyce had just been professed. "How joyfully, how sincerely I congratulate you on the completion of your hopes and wishes." When Sisters were professed at new convents she called them her "grandchildren." But she got steadily worse; and on the 12th of October she dated what is believd to be her last letter. It is quite short.

"My Dear Sister Mary Frances,—Very Rev. Dr

Kirby,* Vice-president of the Irish College at Rome, having called here the day before he sailed, I mentioned to him some evident mistakes in the copy of our Holy Rule; he told me to select them, and forward the document to him, with Archbishop Murray's signature, and said we should, without any more trouble, obtain permission to rectify them. I almost forgot to add, what will occur to yourself, not to speak of any mistakes in the Rule.

"I have just received your welcome letter. How grateful I ought to be for all your anxiety. We shall meet again, *but not at present*. I was sorry to hear poor Dr Fitzgerald is suffering so much. Tell him I pray with all the fervour I can for his comfort, etc.—Ever your affectionate,

MARY C. M'AULAY."

The subject of this letter—the examination of the Rule—was almost the last act of her life. She rallied for a couple of weeks without any near indication of approaching death. "Present at every community exercise when she was scarce able to crawl, it was with difficulty the Sisters persuaded her to allow herself the comfort of retiring an hour before the appointed time." The Sisters could not bring their minds to believe that Catherine M'Aulay would really die; she seemed so indispensable to

---

* In 1889 Monsignor Kirby survived as President of the Irish College in Rome, being then well over ninety years of age. He had a kind welcome and a warm blessing for those who loved Ireland. He lived some few years longer yet, extremely beloved and revered.

them, and to the rapidly spreading Institute. But she herself did not believe that she was indispensable; she knew that it was God's work more than hers, and she had ever taught them that its prosperity did not depend on any individual but on a continuation of His blessing. She herself knew what was coming; she set all in order, and when she had arranged her papers, turning to Sister M. Teresa Carton, she said: "Now they are ready, my child." Calmly she settled all her business as if she were going to be absent a long time; but this excited no alarm, as she always did so before setting out on foundations. After death her papers were found, every one in its own place; the thousands and tens of thousands which had passed through her hands were accounted for to the very farthing, in the clear concise method of bookkeeping which she had adopted; wills, deeds, and legacies, were arranged in order, and an index showed where each item could be found; such of her correspondence, as might not, if produced, prove agreeable to persons still living, and such as was strictly confidential, could not be found, she probably having destroyed it to prevent unpleasant consequences. As far as she could, she made the way easy, as she would say, for her successor, and one could not examine her papers, arrangements, etc., spiritual and temporal, without seeing that "He that feareth God neglecteth nothing."

This was one side of her fine nature, and explains much of the worldly success of the convents founded by her, and how they were enabled to throw off fresh shoots of ever-multiplying usefulness. But her spiritual powers were what attracted young and old to her side. We are told that "all her life she appears to have had a peculiar gift of joy; and during the too short period of her religious life (little more than ten years), she never seemed weary of expatiating on what she called "the joys of her state." "'We *must* be happy,' she said, 'while the spirit of a sublime vocation animates us.' She could not understand sadness in religious. The joy of a good conscience, the joy of spending oneself in the service of Christ, the joy of wearing the livery of such a Master, ought to beam on their very faces she thought. She had seen and mingled with the world during the greater part of her life, and she had seen it under favourable aspects, for her friends and connections were all estimable persons; yet she ever held that if there is true happiness on earth it is found in the religious life by those who are animated by the spirit of their vocation."

This is truly a wonderful testimony; and on the natural sufferings of the last fortnight of her life we will not dwell: her sweet serenity did not fail.

At four in the morning of Thursday, November the 11th, she called the Infirmarian, and said: "My darling, could you have this bed moved to the middle of the room? I shall soon want air."

It was only after she had said this, that the Sisters believed she would never leave that bed alive.

"About seven she said she would like to see the

Sisters individually; and, as each one came, she gave to her the spiritual advice best suited to her individual necessities; but with every one of them she began and ended by inculcating union and charity. 'If you observe the peace and union which have never yet been violated amongst us, you will feel, even in this world, a happiness that will inspire you, and be to you a foretaste of the bliss prepared for every one of you in Heaven.' She sent again for a very old nun, who had nursed a dear nephew, James M'Aulay, on his deathbed; and as if wishing her also to think happily of the death which could not in the course of nature be far off, said to her: 'My fears have all vanished, Sister darling. I feel exceedingly happy.'"

"To the very last she recognised every one that entered the room. Seeing her god-child Teresa (little Sister Camillus) weeping bitterly, she said to her: 'Kiss me, my heart, and then go away; but don't be crying.' It was not easy to obey the last injunction. She had held Teresa at the baptismal font, she had reared and educated her, she had been for years her spiritual mother; how could the poor young Sister restrain her tears when she saw herself about to lose the gentle guardian of her childhood."

Note the sweet familiar Irish of that tender speech. It has a ring like the crooning of an old nurse, rather than that of the reverend Mother.

The end came about eight in the evening. "She continued praying and responding to the prayers for the departing as long as she was able.

Mother Elizabeth from Limerick, an 'old Sister,' who had been specially sent for, having said for her a favourite prayer of hers, she turned her head towards her, and said impressively: 'May God Almighty bless you, my child!' About a quarter to eight, the Sisters, fearing she did not hear the consoling prayers, suggested to Mother Elizabeth, who was reciting them, to raise her voice a little, which she did; but the dying Foundress at once said: 'No occasion to speak so loud, my darling.' Then distinctly, a few minutes before eight, she gave an affectionate blessing to all her children, present and absent, and then calmly closed her eyes to open them no more. Seldom has God summoned from earth a soul so well fitted to deck His paradise."

So died Catherine M'Aulay, having only just attained her fifty-fourth year; having spent about ten years in the religious habit. No portrait of her was ever taken during her life. "After her death a sculptor was employed to take a cast of her features; and a Sister painted in oil a life-size portrait, which is considered tolerably correct, though taken from a corpse." In youth she had been beautiful; a fair woman with blue eyes, and a sweet motherly expression; and "years and sorrows dealt very gently with her beauty." She would probably have lived to old age, if she had allowed herself any sort of luxury. But she wanted to do her work, and did it; and then was ready to go. After her death that work assumed such enormous proportions that, twenty-five years later, the number of convents was over two hundred, and the members of the order over three thousand. Thirty-two years have passed since *that* date, and what the number now are I do not know. The Golden Jubilee was celebrated in 1881, and here and there were aged nuns who had been received by Mrs M'Aulay. It is hardly likely that any of that first band now survive.

At Sunderland, in 1881, one of them was Superioress, and the children took part in a little convent drama, of which the Bishop wrote the words for them. "From the first act—in which Mother M'Aulay is represented kneeling before a crucifix, an angel conveying to her the message that 'Virgins shall follow her, decking God's own Church as lilies deck the eastern meadow fields,' the apparition melting slowly amidst music—till the last scene, in which Mother Catherine is represented in the sleep of death, the interest never flags."

This Bishop had promised the students of Ushaw to be with them on the 17th of May, and he failed not to keep the appointment; for he was carried there in his coffin,—to the college where he had been educated. He was a countryman of Catherine M'Aulay.

My bewildering task is finished, and without any mention of Scotland or the Eastern States. But wherever the English-speaking race has planted its ever-spreading roots, *there* is a convent of the Irish Order of Mercy.

I am enabled to give a short description of the

great hospital ruled by Mother Baptiste Russell in San Francisco. It is written by one familiar to the place, and I add it, as an efficient postscript to the tale.

Market Street, the main thoroughfare of San Francisco, runs its course from the blue waters and crowded shipping of the Bay straight west, until it cuts through the hills that girdle the horizon like a rampart of smooth gold. Down near the Bay, to the south of this great artery, rises Rincon Hill, crowned by the huge red brick pile of the Sisters of Mercy — Saint Mary's Hospital. The immediate surroundings are sullen and sordid. It is set in the midst of the labour of the city, for the help and blessing of those who go up and down in ceaseless toil. The air palpitates with the noise and tumult of great foundries that burn and beat iron into shape for human uses; brisk and fidgety saw-mills cut and rend wood; the ring and din of shipbuilding is carried up from the Potrero; and the air is weighted with the muffled sounds of the loading of ships which carry away the commerce of a most fruitful and blessed land. But once inside the grounds of the Hospital, the noisy sounds of work and busy life give way to a cloistral calm and silence. Upon the very summit of the hill the building rises five storeys above the great stone parapet which supports and props it. From the windows one has in all directions a varied and most beautiful outlook. To the south the waters of San Francisco Bay sweep in an azure glory, until they are lost in the lagoons and marshes of Alviso. To the east the shore of the Bay is flanked by the Berkeley Hills, which hang soft, golden, mysterious, above the towns and villages nestling at their feet. To the north one sees the towers of the Church of St Francis of Assisi cutting the air with a faint and far-fetched memory of Notre Dame de Paris. Beyond are the purple slopes of Tamalpais, and farther still, blue and dim like a dream, above the distant waters flutter the hills of Sonoma and Napa. The city lies to the west, always growing, and stretching, and straggling in uneven streets and ill-cut roads up the slopes of the marvellous line of hills that lie between it and the great wide fields of the Pacific. There is not a window in all of St Mary's that has not for tired eyes a blessing and a panacea; turn which way one will, one has always hills, or sea, or summer skies to cheer one.

MADAME DUCHESNE

Chapter I

"SOLDIER AND MISSIONARY"

It would be a blessing if many of the active pens now working in fiction were used on a more difficult task, that of recording the actual characteristics of people as they were. Since Balzac laid down his last sheet of manuscript, worn out by labour and premature decay, the provincial Frenchwoman who figures in so many of his stories has fallen into comparative oblivion. Very unpleasant portraits of very bad specimens of her race find their way to our shores, but there is no second Balzac to give us another Eugénie Grandet; and the serious, capable woman of the French provinces must be sought for in biography if she is ever to be made real to the English public.

And an initial difficulty confronts the writer. Before people's lives are written they must needs either have done something remarkable or have suffered some terrible fate: to have stabbed Marat in his bath; to have been guillotined alone or with relatives; to have been massacred outside the prison of La Force; to have been married by an heroic soldier and divorced by an emperor,—raises any Frenchwoman to a sort of pedestal for all time; and it is no wonder that the minutest details of such lives should be eagerly read. But to have achieved remarkable results excites a less concentrated interest, and the particular form into which the cleverest and most solid types of the women of France have thrown their lifelong energies requires explanation of the *mise-en-scène*. The special capacity of the provincial women of France (of all ranks) has been drawn out in religious and charitable work. They have supplied brains as well as heart to those who lacked strength in the competition of life. There are no workhouses in France, and no great pauper population. When the horse stumbles and the waggoner falls from his seat, there is, metaphorically speaking, generally a Frenchwoman about, ready to pick him up. She is the one great helpful reserve of power. If anything very bad occurs, the French people do not rush for a policeman in a cocked hat, they rush for a nun, and whether or no they themselves are imbued with sentiments of piety, they invariably expect *her* to be all there!

And these women as a whole come from the farming and trading classes. Jeanne Rendu, who was buried in 1859 with the Cross of the Legion of Honour on her coffin, and a *peloton* of soldiers firing over her grave, came from the Jura mountains; Sophie Madeleine Barat was the daughter of "a worthy hard-working artisan" in the little town of Joigny in Burgundy. She was born in 1779, and, eighty years afterwards, Montalembert records that he had "to-day seen for the first time the famous Madame Barat" led into the parlour between two Sisters who supported her feeble steps.

HISTORIC NUNS

The life and work of Madame Barat is well known in London and Paris, through the great educational convents of the Sacred Heart. Her biography is most accessible. That of her dear friend and fellow-worker, Rose Philippine Duchesne, is rather less known, as the second part of it belongs to the Western World. It is to be found in the British Museum, but not as yet in the Bodleian Library, where the name is represented by a certain Père Duchesne, not unknown to revolutionary history.

Madame Duchesne has serious claims to fame, and was cousin-german of a man of much mark in the early part of this century, the politician and financier, Casimir Périer the First.

The Duchesnes had been solidly established for a number of years at Romans in the Drôme, and had acquired wealth and position as manufacturers of stuffs which they sold and forwarded to every part of France and her colonies. In 1769 the grandfather of this little girl whose history is well worth re-telling, appears to have been still living. He had married one Mademoiselle Marie Louise Enfantin, and had two sons, the eldest of whom carried on his father's business, while the younger one, Pierre François, went to the Bar. They were citizens of Grenoble, which was the seat of a provincial Parliament. Pierre was a man of brilliant ability, and he married a rich heiress in the same solid rank of life. The Périers had been well known in commercial circles before they became eminent in the Parisian world; they were near neighbours and old friends when Rose Euphrosine Périer became Pierre François Duchesne's wife. When little Rose Philippine was baptised, her sponsors were her grandmother, Madame Jacques Périer, and her maternal Uncle Jean.

The dwellings of the two families were side by side in the Place St André at Grenoble, and may probably be still extant. They are described as being just opposite to the church of that name, and to the Gothic palace of the Counts of Dauphiné, transformed into the Palais de Justice. A covered passage led from the street into the inner court of the Maison Duchesne. "The grand staircase, the monastic appearance of the windows, grated like those of a convent, and the solemn aspect of the court into which they look, give a correct idea of the austere and modest mode of existence of wealthy merchants of the olden time." A door of communication between the houses of the two families was visible late in this century, though walled up.

Here the young child grew, under the tuition of her mother, who is described as a thoroughly valiant woman, inheriting the vigour of intellect inherent in the Périer family. When she was old enough to go to school she was sent to a convent of the Visitation on a high mountain slope overlooking Grenoble, called by the picturesque name of Ste Marie-d'en-Haut. As this building played a great part in Philippine Duchesne's history, it shall be fully described. "A steep winding street, lined on both sides by dismal-looking houses, dating from the time of the League, leads to a sudden turning, opposite to which stands an archway, surmounted by the following inscription:—

"St François de Sales chose this place for the foundation of the fourth monastery of his Order of the Visitation of St Mary. The first stone of it was laid in his presence on October 16, 1619."

Here came Madame de Chantal, the grandmother of Madame de Sevigné, canonised as St Jeanne Françoise de Chantal; and here the Duc de Lesdiguières had adorned a large church with a marble altar, and carved pulpit, and sculptured stalls, and with a frescoed roof, which recorded the mysteries of the Gospel and the origin of the convent. The size and splendour of some of the provincial churches in France is particularly exemplified by that of Grignan, before whose altar Madame de Sevigné herself lies buried. From a village street and the door of a modest Presbytère, the traveller may pass into a building which recalls the churches of Versailles. From the terrace of Ste Marie-d'en-Haut, which was the children's playground, was, and is still to be seen, "the whole of the rich valley of Grésivaudau, which embraces the most picturesque variety of natural beauty, backed by the snow-capped summits of the Alps."

In this grand old place little Philippine grew up to girlhood, and there she was brought in contact with a priest who had been labouring in Louisiana, and told the children stories about the savages. She was only eight years old when her little head and heart were possessed with the idea that it must be "a great happiness to be a missionary." And the horrible stories of Jesuit Fathers who had been shot, scalped, and cut in pieces only excited her to envy! None of these things ever happened to Philippine; but the certain fact that she thought this at eight years old to be a remarkably happy lot, had the most extraordinary and, in the end, practical results.

Philippine's uncle, Claude Périer, had eight sons, and he kept them "hard at their books, under the care of a learned priest," in a square turret still to be seen; and when the girl came home (owing to a fear on the part of her parents that she wanted to become a nun), she asked to attend the boys' lessons, and gave herself to Latin and arithmetic. She "studied music likewise but without success. The most remarkable of her gifts when a young woman was that of writing—a gift, not an art— for her style was always irregularly natural and spontaneous, but sometimes hardly grammatical. Strength and power mark it with a sort of rough energy akin to the ardent soul and iron will which distinguished her."

When Philippine was seventeen years of age proposals of marriage had already been made for a younger sister; and her father and mother thought it proper to begin by finding a husband for her, as the elder. They proposed a suitable match, but Philippine was not inclined to matrimony. She managed to overcome the opposition of her parents, and at eighteen became a postulant. We are told that there were other unmarried daughters, and even "a new little sister born that year." The sisters and their children play a considerable part in Philippine's life, although she was so early devoted to the savages and St Francis Xavier, whom she used to ask to call her away by some special summons.

But though Philippine had entered the convent she was still a very long way from taking the veil. Her father, the advocate, was "by no means a pious man," but he had enough respect for religion, which was then a vital power in such families as that of the Duchesnes, not to oppose his daughter's will on the point, had not public affairs been just then in a very alarming state. "Nothing could be more dark and threatening than their aspect. Philippine was herself but too well aware of the important events which were occurring almost under her eyes, and in which her own relatives had participated. It was in her native city, and almost under her father's roof, that the first revolutionary steps had been taken."

In June 1788 the Parliament of Grenoble had issued a proclamation against certain royal edicts. Blood flowed in the streets of the old town. "It was the first battle of the French Revolution."

This is not the place in which to discuss the tangled beginnings of the changes which swept over France. The Duchesnes and Périers appear to have been Liberals of the educated old-fashioned sort; but the storm which none of them foresaw, and which had been so long brewing, broke with violence all over France. The nuns of the Visitation were expelled from St Marie-d'en-Haut, and there was for years an end of Philippine's projects. She begged to be allowed to go to a convent in Italy, but her parents would not consent to her departure, and she retired with them to a country-house at Granne, not far from the town of Romans, and there they appear to have been practically unmolested for some few years—terrible years in Paris and other great centres of French population. There are few details of the life led at Granne, but a letter from Philippine to her sister, Madame de Mauduit (addressed to Citoyenne Mauduit), alludes to the death of their mother, Madame Pierre François Duchesne, who died in her arms comforted and supported to the last. Their father's "business agent" at his mills, which he seems to have kept going, was none other than a priest, the good Abbé Poidebard, who had barely escaped the guillotine, and now worked for his own support and assisted the family by the exercise of his sacred ministry. He "said mass by night in the most secluded parts of the house."

At the mother's death Philippine came into landed property, which she gave up to her brothers and sisters in return for a small annuity. She wrote to one of her sisters thus: "After a great misfortune had placed me in possession of a fortune, I thought the best way to enjoy it was to give it up. Heavenly hopes were what I kept for my portion. I wish this letter to bear witness against me if questions of interest were ever to divide us, and if I did not show myself ready to enter into whatever arrangements you consider most to your advantage."

The next episode in Philippine's life was her sojourn with an impossible grandmother—on the father's side. This good lady carried to the most despairing degree the intractable wilfulness of the Duchesne character. She quarrelled with her tenants and servants from morning till night, and her granddaughter was greatly relieved at being dismissed at the end of a few weeks. Here are the sage remarks she made to Madame de Mauduit: "In observing the change which advancing years have made in our grandmothers, I cannot refrain, dear sister, from some melancholy thoughts. We are of the same race, and already often feel in ourselves symptoms of their impetuous disposition. How much I fear that the resemblance may increase in time, and make us one day the bane and the torment of our families." Some softly-worded sentences followed this reflection; and we learn that the lady to whom they were thus ingenuously addressed was much in need of them, for though Madame de Mauduit was a kind-hearted and most charitable person, and specially attentive to the sick, tradition likewise reports that she was terribly imperious. Her husband, a peaceable captain of dragoons, who had preserved the courteous style and manners of the old *régime*, suffered from her *brusquerie*. He used to say that he could more easily rule his soldiers than his wife, and he was not suffered often to make the latter attempt.

Meantime Philippine's youth was passing away,

and she remained as fixed as ever in her desire to embrace the religious life if only it were possible. She made a journey to Grenoble, some time apparently in the year 1793; and climbed up the steep hill to the beloved old convent where she had been educated. "It had been turned into a prison, and was at that moment crowded with victims awaiting execution. Among them were ladies of rank": Madame de Brissac and others; men of old name, M. de Gramont Caderousse, for instance; venerable nuns like Madame Peret, foundress of the Ursulines of Grenoble, and several priests. M. Revenas, formerly Curé of Tolissieux, in the diocese of Gex, was here shut up, with a companion, Joseph Martin Guillabert. When the latter was told that a mass had been secretly offered up for him, he said: "The Blood of the Lamb offered up for me makes me ashamed of hesitating to shed mine." M. Revenas, when removed from Ste Marie-d'en-Haut to the cellars of the Conciergerie, called them the ante-chambers of Paradise. He died on the scaffold on the 26th of June 1794, and his last words were, "Blessed be Jesus, for Whom I die! I give Him back life for life and love for love." In the midst of the prison life, Philippine Duchesne was unwearied in carrying succour and consolation, and her relatives were terrified lest she herself should be arrested, and her life be the forfeit.

At last came the turn of the tide; and when France began to breathe freely and make efforts towards social recovery, the male members of the Duchesne family took an active part in the crisis. They were efficient men of business, and highly intelligent. In 1795, the brothers-in-law, Claude Périer and Pierre François Duchesne, were elected deputies to the legislative body in Paris. The latter ardently opposed the *coup d'état* of the 18th Brumaire. With Carnot, he voted against the life-consulate of Napoleon, "and, when vanquished in the struggle, returned to Grenoble, convinced that there was an end of liberty for France, but unchanged in his convictions."

It is interesting to trace the double strain in this family: the strong sense of the men enabling them to measure the forces of that resistless modern current which the Revolution had set free, and the religious fervour which swayed Rose Philippine and two of her nieces to carry out their own will, and finally to plant great educational institutions in the United States. For to America the course of the narrative is leading us.

It was in 1801, when Mademoiselle Duchesne was thirty-two years of age, that she saw her way to purchase the deserted building of Ste Marie-d'en-Haut. "It had been declared the property of the nation, and remained uninhabited, except that the man placed there to take charge of it used on Sundays to turn it into a sort of public-house for the people who made the mountain a promenade." On the Whitsunday of that year she went to visit it, taking with her her young motherless sister and her little niece of three years old, Amelie de

Mauduit. As they stood on the terrace, she was surprised to hear the child say, as she rolled on the thick grass which was growing there in rank abundance, "Oh yes; I shall come to school here, and I shall make my first Communion here." It must be remembered that school and first Communion were among the very first words ever heard by the children of the Duchesne and Périer families, and would be caught up by their little tongues long before the true meaning of the words could be understood. The result of this visit was that Mademoiselle Duchesne set to work to obtain the great empty premises, and as her cousins Périer were much thought of in Paris, and exerted themselves in her behalf, she was able to obtain a lease of it from the Government, at a rent of 800 francs yearly (about £32), and an engagement to put it in good repair. This was just at the time when First Consul Bonaparte was on the point of making the Concordat with the Pope.

It would be too long for the purpose of these pages to detail how Mademoiselle Duchesne struggled for more than a year to re-open Ste Marie-d'en-Haut on something of its old lines. She failed, and in August 1802 she sat alone in the great house, crying like "the holy women of the Gospel near an empty sepulchre." She could not see her way at all. Community life in France had been shattered and disorganised for ten years. Yet on that very day a certain friendly priest, the Rev. Jean Baptiste Rivet, came to see her, as she sat weeping with disappointment, and he told her of a religious congregation lately founded at the very distant town of Amiens, which he held in the highest esteem.

The head of that little house was a young nun, just ten years younger than Philippine herself, and daughter of an artisan and *cultivateur*. She it was whom Montalembert, sixty years later, spoke of as "the famous Madame Barat," whom he visited in her extreme old age; and when, after lengthy negotiations, this youthful Superior, accompanied by three other nuns, arrived at Ste Marie to take possession of it in the name of the Sacred Heart, Mademoiselle Duchesne came down the steps to meet her and knelt at her feet, kissing them, with the salutation: "How beautiful upon the mountains are the feet of Him that bringeth good tidings and preacheth peace"; and a great and holy friendship was begun between two women whose works are now a monument to French piety in the Eastern and in the Western world—on the banks of the Thames, as on those of the Mississippi and the Seine.

Up to this time it must be remarked that Mademoiselle Duchesne had never been able to realise her early purpose of herself becoming a nun, one obstacle after another had interfered, but at the age of five-and-thirty she re-entered the novitiate at Ste Marie-d'en-Haut, now fully assigned to the welcome strangers, and in due time was professed, becoming one of the regular community under Madame Barat. Her interior and exterior experiences at this epoch are well worth reading, but they form part of the story of the planting of the new order in Paris and elsewhere. Nevertheless, so far as she was personally concerned, she clung with unwearying perseverance to her early purpose of converting savages; she spoke of them as "black," never having seen a savage in her life; but it was the dispossessed tribes of Red Indians after whom she really aspired. It was they, through the recitals of the missionary priests, or possibly through the pages of Chateaubriand, who had fired her youthful fancy. She consulted priests innumerable, and besieged Madame Barat for leave and approbation, in hopeful longing for a journey to what was then indeed the wild West. And this sounded the more extraordinary because the work of the order had rapidly developed in educational channels, and year by year it was assuming the shape it still possesses, and bestowing its splendid energies on great schools for girls of the upper classes, who had certainly no interest in redskin Indians, and to whom missionary ardour was as a rule unknown.

However, no Duchesne ever relinquished a purpose or failed to get hold of its practical link. The discreet priest who writes the biography half reveals and half conceals the way in which this tormenting member of the saintly family prayed and persuaded while rigorously fulfilling the day's duties. Says Madame Barat, writing to another nun: "Your good Mother Duchesne teaches in the schools all day, sits up at night with the sick children in the infirmary, has the whole exterior management of the house, and never seems distressed and scarcely overworked. What a valiant woman." Even so, but while recognising to the full the high and shining powers of Mother Duchesne's nature, we find Madame Barat most unwilling to authorise the start in the New World. It was a serious question whether so young a society would not be too much weakened by widely disseminating the elements of which it was composed. And so year after year passed on; the one nun catching hold of every clue relating to the States of America or the pagan countries of the East, the other calmer woman, who was in the position of authority, puzzled and sometimes pained at her friend's insistence, and urging: " I cannot understand how a person of sound sense can let herself be so carried away by her imagination as not to consider what are the means to the end." Nevertheless, she somewhat relents, and tells Madame Duchesne that one of the priests of St Sulpice, a generous-hearted and clever man, though harsh in manner, in whom they both had great confidence, had been speaking about her, and that she herself had felt a sort of pleasure in seeing how much interest he took in the subject of her plans. "In that peculiar way of his which makes me believe in all his utterances as if they were articles of faith, he said that you were not to give up your hopes, but only to become more humble, more obedient, more mortified, and resigned to the will of God in a calm, quiet manner, and that our Lord would make known to you what will be most pleasing to him."

It was not until the year 1818, when Mother

Duchesne was nearly fifty years old, that the way at last opened for the fulfilment of her life-long wish.

She had gone to Paris on the business of the new house which had been opened in the Rue des Postes, near Sainte Geneviève, and which, when transferred to the Rue de Varennes, became the centre of the world-wide work of the order, and here she came across the Superior of the Foreign Missions, who had showed her letters from China, and related the martyrdom of a Bishop in Sutchen; and about the same time, indeed a little earlier, she had heard of a missionary priest who had recently been made Bishop of New Orleans. Here was a chance, indeed! His name was Monsignor Dubourg, and he had come over to France to beat up recruits for his diocese, and to get money for his various works. He had been preaching in Lyons with extraordinary success. Thus when the new Bishop came to call on Madame Barat at the Rue des Postes, the nuns were familiar with his name. Madame Duchesne happened to be portress, and it was she who went to announce his visit to Madame Barat, and, quoth she: " Now is the hour of Providence ! I do beseech of you, Reverend Mother, not to miss the opportunity. You have only a word to say. I implore you say it." During that first interview nothing was, however, said; but next morning, after he had said mass in their convent chapel, and while Madame Barat was sitting with him during his breakfast, the Bishop began to talk to her of America, and one of the first things he said was how glad he should be to establish in his diocese Sisters of the Sacred Heart, and he earnestly begged her to give him some of her nuns.

The excellent man had really alighted like a heavenly visitant on that little new convent. Wings could not have made him more welcome. Everything was to come about naturally and reasonably. It required a prudent, hard-working Bishop to convince the equally prudent Madame Barat, by this time forty years of age, that she could trust her incalculable Philippine in those strange regions—Philippine who must have been growing grey with the passion of hope deferred. And so the matter was settled, and Monsignor Dubourg was to go in advance of the nuns, and they were to follow across that wild waste of waters, and be probably received at New Orleans. And Father Barat, the very austere brother of Madame Barat, wrote a letter of congratulation, saying with a touch of irony: "So at last all is settled, and you are going to work among the Illinois! You had set your heart on the Iroquois, but have had to descend a few hundred miles lower. You are not quite holy enough to be eaten up by the Hurons and Algonquins. Thank God, you will not yet be devoured by the savages, but you must be eaten up by the love of God, and a fiery zeal for souls. Ask of God that he who writes to you may be sent also to those missions. He would be delighted to go, his Superiors know it, and if you have an opportunity you may remind them of it."

On the 27th of June the Bishop embarked at

Bordeaux on a small ship of the Royal Navy which Louis the Eighteenth had placed at his disposal; and Madame Duchesne wrote to tell her relatives of her approaching departure. Her relations with her two married sisters, Madame de Mauduit and Madame Jouve, had always been close and affectionate; together they had nursed their father, Pierre François Duchesne on his deathbed, four years previously, and had brought him round, after a lifetime of eighteenth-century philosophy, to the sacraments of the Church. Philippine had done all she could to increase their inheritance; she had cherished their children, and she had hoped to have been accompanied by one of the daughters of Madame Jouve, who had been educated at Ste Marie-d'en-Haut, and had joined the community. But Aloysia's health had failed, and that sacrifice was to be added to the rest. To Madame de Mauduit, Philippine wrote: "Rely upon it, dearest sister, I shall always be closely united with you, and will continually pray for you, your husband, your son and your daughter." And to Madame Jouve even yet more tenderly: "I shall leave France this month, but I carry away with me all my recollections of home, all my affection for my dear sisters and their children. You will pray for me and I shall pray for you. At this moment, when I am leaving everything behind in order to work for the salvation of a few souls, I feel the most intense desire that you may cling to the one thing that is necessary. I am, and shall ever be, devotedly yours in the Sacred Heart of Jesus."

Several nuns came forward and offered to share

the fatigues and dangers which loomed large in the imagination of Frenchwomen in the beginning of this century. One of them was a young Sister from Geneva. Octavie Berthold was daughter to the private secretary of Voltaire. She was a convert to Catholicism when past twenty years of age. She must be called the first volunteer for the American Mission by the side of Philippine Duchesne. The second recruit was of a very different sort. Mademoiselle Eugénie Audé had lived in the best society of Piedmont and Tuscany, and had been presented at the Court of the Emperor Napoleon. She had been devoted to dress and amusements, and was quite a worldly young person. But like many another she had changed in mid-career, had taken the veil at Ste Marie-d'en-Haut, and had then been transferred to Paris, and on to a new foundation at Quimper in Brittany. She was recalled to Paris to make her final vows before departing on the foreign missions, whither she had asked to go. She was very clever, and rendered the greatest services in the American schools. She is described as being particularly attached to Madame Barat, whom she had learnt to know and love when in Paris with an intense affection, which during all her life was a source of strength and consolation, but also of suffering to her heart. She was the only one of the three who after some years returned to France. Two lay Sisters begged to be allowed also to serve Jesus Christ in those distant countries. Thus the little party contained five ardent souls. The names of the lay Sisters were Catherine Lamarre and

Marguerite Manteau. Madame Duchesne was named Superior of the colony, with exceptional powers for the government of the American province.

Of the farewell scene what can be told! America was then such a weary long way off—so many weeks away—and these five women were going with no intention of return. Madame Barat gave the string of her cross and also her watch to Eugénie Audé, and other things to the rest. They knelt round her, and Madame Duchesne kissed Madame Barat's feet. Those two, so different, had worked long years together; the one had possessed wealth and education, the other had come from a labouring home, yet this last was the ruling spirit. She said, "If you only established one new tabernacle in Louisiana, if you make those poor savages make but one act of love for our Lord, ought you not to consider yourselves greatly blest?"

And round Madame Duchesne her own family gathered as her departure drew near. Some of them had deprecated her leaving France. Her sisters evidently felt severely the loss of her loving, self-sacrificing presence, and the men of her family —merchants, financiers, and politicians — busy in Dauphiné and in Paris, belonged to the Liberal group who were ultimately to rise to power under the Orleans Dynasty, and could hardly be supposed particularly devoted to missionary enterprise. But she refers to them in various of her letters as invariably giving the order their practical support with the Government, and they now furnished the little colony with letters of recommendation to the French Minister and Consul in the United States. They all belonged to what is called in France "la haute bourgeoise," and one of them, Casimir Périer the First, four years later, acted as best man (*témoin*) at the marriage of Louise Swanton with Hilaire Belloc, an eminent French artist under the Restoration. Casimir Périer the Third succeeded Carnot as President of the present French Republic.

On the day of their departure Father Varin and Father Barat came to give the emigrant nuns encouragement and blessing. The former had been for many years Sophie Barat's great support. An interesting account of him is to be found in her Life. Once a brilliant, worldly young officer, he had renounced the army to become a priest, and it was he who had negotiated the transference of Ste Marie-d'en-Haut. He had had, from the time of his first seeing her there, the highest opinion of Philippine Duchesne. He "discerned the greatness of her soul"; and when he got back to Amiens, where he had left Madame Barat, he told her that when she took her colony of Sisters to Grenoble she would find companions already there who would be a help to her, and "one especially—if there were only that one—she would be worth seeking at the other end of the world," and "that one" he was now, after many years had passed, sending away to a far distance never to return. The two dear nuns were never to meet again until both their living earthly times were ended.

And now the moment had arrived. "When,

after a hasty meal, the carriage was announced, Madame Duchesne rose and received a final embrace from her Superior, and also from all the members of the community; she cheered them by her parting words, and cut short the farewell scene. Octavie Berthold was crying, and could hardly tear herself away from the arms of her companions. Madame Duchesne took her hand and drew her out into the carriage. A few moments afterwards they were rolling away in the diligence on the road to Bordeaux, where they were to embark."

The four travellers (they picked up Margaret Manteau at the seaport) slept several times on the way, at Orléans, at Tours, and at Angoulême. Those long journeys along the endless straight roads of France were to be necessary modes of travel for thirty more years. The transcriber of this story remembers them well. When they reached Bordeaux they lodged in the house of a little teaching community directed by Madame Vincent, who had once similarly received Madame Barat, and here they had to wait many days, for their departure depended on the wind. Father Barat appears to have followed them to Bordeaux. He was a very determined and austere priest, who spared neither himself nor anybody else; and Madame Audé said: "If the only grace I had obtained on this journey was that of seeing a saint, I should not regret having taken it."

While thus waiting they received an encouraging communication from a priest in Paris, the Abbé Perreau, with whom Madame Duchesne had left a very private special letter for Madame Barat, detailing some spiritual experiences in reference to the call she herself had so long felt to be imperative; and the Abbé, after telling her that the Superior had been pleased with it, adds that, "on account of the obstacles and opposition which many ecclesiastics had made to the projected journey, he had written to explain the matter at Rome, and to ask the Holy Father's blessing for Madame Duchesne and her companions."

Another very touching letter may be mentioned. Madame de Mauduit, generous, ardent, and not always easy to get on with, had with difficulty been reconciled to losing her sister, who, during the long waiting at Bordeaux, wrote most lovingly: "I was sure that the resolution I have taken would not interfere with that affectionate intimacy between us which has been the delight of my life, and which now gives merit to my sacrifice. To incur dangers is nothing in comparison with the interruption of a close and holy friendship; but it will not really be interrupted, it will continue to exist, and will live on privations." To Madame Jouve she wrote in the same strain, and to the nuns at Ste Marie-d'en-Haut she addressed "heart-stirring words of farewell." Thus they flowed from that ardent, vigorous pen just eighty years ago, and they may well stir the heart to-day: " Dearest friends and children, at the moment when I am leaving all things, almost as really as if I were dying, for it is next to certain that I shall not see you again on earth, any more than so many other mothers, sisters, relatives, and friends, I feel as if I could venture to ask great things from God with that trust which made St Peter say: 'Behold we have left all things and followed Thee, what then shall we have?' Oh! the reward which I implore Him to grant me is the inexpressible consolation of hearing that you are all fervent in His love, that you do good works, and thus advance in that solid piety, the end of which is the enjoyment of God in this world by His grace and in the next by His glory." And to Mother Theresa, a special friend of her own, who had been her companion at Ste Marie-d'en-Haut, she wrote in a still higher tone of ardent self-devotion. "Oh! how I long to go on board that ship which is to carry me to the object of my hopes. But the ties which bind me to the beloved ones I leave in France and to the Society, will become even stronger and closer when I shall have the consolation of working to extend the latter in the New World, and of seeing the devotion to the Sacred Heart flourishing there. . . . As to the prospect of ever seeing you again, I have little hope of it. You are doing good in France, and if Aloysia" (her own niece) "is meant to work elsewhere you will have to part with her." But the young Aloysia was ill, and could not go, and Madame Duchesne at the moment of setting sail wrote her a letter of love and consolation.

At last, on March the 13th, Holy Thursday, the five nuns were accompanied to the place of embarkation by M. Dubourg and Madame Fournier, brother and sister of the Bishop of Louisiana. They got into a boat, which took them down the Garonne to Royan, where they found the ship in which they were to sail. Good Friday they spent on board. "On Holy Saturday the *Rebecca* sailed out of port. The Sisters gave their letters to the coast pilot, and on Easter Day Madame Duchesne lost sight of her native land, which she was never to see again."

They were many weeks on that voyage; it was not till the 25th of May that the *Rebecca* "entered the muddy waters of the Mississippi." And in the intervening days they had been tossed lamentably in the Bay of Biscay, and a proposition was made by somebody at dinner to cast lots in order to find out "which of the passengers was drawing down on the vessel the wrath of heaven. This vexed us, because people at Bordeaux had assured the captain that if priests and nuns sailed in his vessel it would certainly be wrecked." Then on the 21st of April they met an "American corsair," manned by 120 sailors, and armed with eleven cannons. It was on the lookout for Spanish ships, the United States being at that time at war with that country. But the captain of the *Rebecca* was "fortunately an American," and kept them undevoured. In the first days of May the *Rebecca* was "driven by stress of weather five times backwards and forwards across the tropics." The 10th—Pentecost—was passed in a fearful storm. Among the passengers were three poor workmen from Geneva, whom want had driven from their homes, and who hoped to earn a livelihood in New Orleans. As they neared Cuba they met several ships on their way to Europe, and one of them took charge of a letter from Madame Duchesne to Madame Barat. It must not be supposed that it contained nothing but horrors. The dear traveller had seen the "wonderful works of God" upon the sea;—splendid skies, porpoises, and flying-fish, and myriads of polypi "spread over the sea like living flowers." Only one of the lay Sisters, Catherine Lamarre (who lived long and did great work in America) "was quite bewildered, and said she had not thought they were going so far." The other lay Sister, Margaret Manteau, had a beautiful voice, and sang the Ave Maria Stella in a way which charmed and comforted everyone. This hymn was supposed to have the power of obtaining fine weather, and when a storm seemed blowing up, the captain used to call for it!

And now at last the exiles were landed on the soil of America. They took four days to ascend those slow waters of the river to a point six leagues below New Orleans. It was on Friday the 24th of May, towards sunset, when they were making up their minds to spend another night on the ship, that two carriages appeared on the river bank, and two priests sent from the city to welcome the Abbé Martial (the Vicar-General of Mgr. Dubourg), and the five nuns. Eugénie Audé describes the landing, and how Madame Duchesne knelt on the ground and kissed it, saying: "No one is looking at us, kiss it too." And then they set off. It was a beautiful starry night; the bright, dark heaven was reflected in the river, and a multitude of fire-flies danced in the bushes. They passed pretty houses, and one of them stopped to buy some bread. "It was seventy days since we had eaten any. Everything tended to raise our souls to God. Oh! if they could be directed to Him constantly, with a practical desire to promote His glory, we should indeed be happy." And happy they were, these five valiant Frenchwomen. There is no mistaking the cheerful zeal which animated their pens and shines in every sentence.

They were hospitably taken in by the Ursuline nuns, whose Superior, Madame Gensoul, was of their own kind nationality. She and her band of Sisters lived in a convent which had been founded in the eighteenth century, before the purchase of Louisiana from the French. They had originally had a hard time amidst the marshes and uncultivated lands around the Mississippi; but now they were prosperous, and educated almost all the young girls in Lower Louisiana. In the convent more than three hundred girls received a Christian education. Some were rich, and some were poor; but what particularly delighted Madame Duchesne, was to find there a number of little black negresses. If not exactly "savages," they were the next best! However, Madame Duchesne, whose days even then made up half-a-century, was not to escape unscathed from so long a voyage. The lack of vegetables during those long weeks upon the sea had had the usual effect, and as she felt very ill, she took it as a sign that she was called upon to resign her post. "I thought that this was a sign that God required nothing more of me. My feeling was that Eugénie would steer the ship, and that it would gain by the change. I had been more fortunate than Moses, for I was allowed to enter the promised land, and had brought to it the colony which was to do battle for the Sacred Heart. I assure you that the thought of dying was very pleasing to me, for I have every reason to fear that if I live I shall spoil the work of our foundation."

But the kind Ursulines administered baths and refreshing drinks, and an excellent change of food; and Madame Duchesne got well, and was obliged to relinquish her cheerful vision of being a second Moses. Her whole nature was so ardent and original that there is no end in her biography of the strange and touching twists and turns of her spiritual life. She dwelt on a plane which rendered her absolutely indifferent to self. In the moral life she may be compared to one inhabiting a fourth dimension.

She was greatly rejoiced to see every evening the blacks and mulattoes who gathered round the Abbé Martial to learn the catechism; and she even had the exquisite pleasure of intercourse with a few Indians—" in all probability the last remnant of the tribe of Choctaws—who inhabited a village on the other side of the lake, Pontchartrain." She grieved at their sad and miserable expression. They called the nuns "the women of the Great Spirit"; and the name "seemed an appeal, and roused her zeal to the utmost."

Madame Duchesne had to wait several months with the Ursulines for a letter from the Bishop, who on arriving had preceded them to St Louis; and though he wrote a letter of welcome, it in some strange way miscarried. The Ursuline nuns wanted them to stay in New Orleans and found a school of their own; but for that the time was not yet come, and "having heard in an indirect manner that Monsignor Dubourg was expecting her at St Louis, Madame Duchesne made up her mind to set off for that place." So the Ursuline nuns made them a present of 1500 francs (£60), and the five travellers again set off on the steamer *Franklin*. Their Superior observes that steamboats are "an admirable invention which enables people to accomplish in twenty days what used to be two years ago a business of six months." And this, be it observed, was written just eighty years ago. But even so, there was no end to the delays, though the distance between New Orleans and St Louis is only 1300 miles, and the railway now takes thirty-six hours. The travellers were, of course, making their way up stream, and they encountered sand banks and snags; almost every day some accident occurred; once it took nineteen hours to disengage the steamer; another time the fuel fell short, and they came to a dead stop, and every one went on shore and "picked up wood in the primeval forest." Their bread ran out, and they pounded ears of maize into flour. At a place called Ascension they picked up a French priest who was "the celebrated M. Gabriel Richard, a native of Saintes, in the west of France, and a great-nephew of the great Bossuet on the mother's side. M. Richard had that year been elected a member of the American Congress."

From one cause or another the journey up the Great River lasted forty-two days, until at last the little band reached St Louis, then a small town of 6000 inhabitants, founded about fifty years earlier. Madame Duchesne lived to see it shelter 150,000. It was not, however, at St Louis that the first definite beginning was made. After a rest of three weeks the Bishop sent them a few leagues farther up the river to a smaller settlement called St Charles. The truth was that neither the Bishop nor Madame Duchesne had any money except the sums sent to them across the vast Atlantic. The Bishop himself, who had landed at a port called Annapolis, had literally gone on foot through Maryland and Pennsylvania at the head of a band of priests he had collected in France, and taken boat at Pittsburg, acting as master and pilot. When at length he reached St Louis, he sent off the priests to different parts of the immense diocese;—a diocese made up of forests, rivers, marshes, and widely-scattered settlements. And when the nuns came to him up stream he sent them away also, putting them in a small hired house; here Madame Duchesne feared that nothing could ever be planned for the work of which she had hoped so much. Said she, with her customary picturesque energy of speech: "I listened to him like a rock into which holes were being bored. I go on with closed eyes, if it be God's will. Providence will open a way. My Sisters are more courageous and fervent than I am. They look at the Cross and they embrace it." The Bishop did not spare his own trouble. He put the five nuns in a vehicle, and rode on horseback by the side, and helped his charges across the river.

HISTORIC NUNS

The good men who carried their baggage refused to receive a penny for their trouble, and said that priests and nuns were to them living pictures of our Lord Jesus Christ. So Monsignor planted his countrywomen in a little home of five rooms, with a rather larger one in the middle. It was evidently built of wood, as all the inhabitants of the place (about 500 families) lived in wooden cabins. They were people of mixed races—French and Canadians, Germans, Irish, half-caste savages, and negroes. Hunters of the prairies, trappers and adventurers of every kind, passed across St Charles; and families of labourers with their wives and children. And in this motley place the nuns had to collect a school, and to provide for their own sustenance by keeping cows. Then came the winter cold—so intense that the water froze close by the fire, and linen placed before it grew stiff. The bread failed, and when the river was frozen over the nuns were reduced to a slender provision of maize, potatoes, and salt fish. Their only oil was "bear's oil."

They struggled through twelve months under these appalling difficulties; and they taught many interesting children, whom they were most loath to leave. But their lives would have been risked by a second such winter, and they and their scanty goods were transferred to a place called Fleurissant, on the other side of the Missouri. But the cows were so indignant at being tied, and the heat was now so great (it was the 3rd of September 1819) that they waited till the cool of the morning, and then persuaded the cows by dint of cabbages. But no sooner were the beasts across (in company with all the hens), and the ropes untied, than they made a rush for the woods, the priest of the new parish galloping after them.

Fleurissant, now a pretty country place, was then "a boundless expanse of waving grass, where the savage tribe of the Sioux used to encamp," and there a small settlement of huts and (wooden) houses had been made. The galloping priest was M. l'Abbé Delacroix, a Belgian by birth, who, when studying for the priesthood, had been drafted into the army of Napoleon. When Bishop Dubourg made an appeal for missionaries for Louisiana, Charles Delacroix had volunteered. He now gave up his own house to the five nuns and two pupils, and "was living in a hut like a bird-cage. It was one of the cabins made of matting in which the emigrants hung up the maize to dry, and the good priest crept into it through its only hole." He fell ill of a fever, and the Bishop had a "really good" abode made for him, solidly built of "old planks." As to the Convent, it was a farm, and the Frenchwomen lived as farm servants. The winter was again very severe, and when the ever-lively cows ran away, the nuns followed them through snow, bush, and briar. Nevertheless, at Fleurissant they managed to make a real start, and in May 1820 they had a house built of bricks, and twenty-one pupils.

Nothing in the strange narrative is more touching than the way in which they maintained communication with France. Madame Barat contrived to get money sent across to them—money contributed by friends in the outer world. Madame Duchesne's brother offered to send her money to bring her back to France. "Tell him," she said, "that I beg of him to give that sum for the travelling expenses of two more nuns for Louisiana."

At Fleurissant Madame Duchesne remained for several years, always struggling with material difficulties, and obliged to part with her most capable assistant, Madame Audé, who was sent to found a school near the Gulf of Mexico. This establishment, named the Grand Coteau, was not far from a settlement named the Opelusas. The Grand Coteau, as its name implies, was a ridge overlooking marshes and prairies, which finally stretched out to the Gulf. It was at that time partly covered by the primeval forest; and watercourses, offshoots of the Mississippi, intersected the land in all directions. The scene was "majestic, but also melancholy in the extreme; and here one Mr Charles Smith had made a plantation of cotton and sugar canes with slave labour. The estate was 142 acres in extent." Mr Smith naturally made a large fortune, and he built houses for his two brothers, whom he invited to live near him. He and his wife were Catholics, and he planned a settlement which was to include houses of education for boys and girls. He, however, died before he had completed the buildings. He had finished the church, and then left half his fortune and his unfinished wishes to his widow. She carried them out loyally, but the negotiations bring the reader into quite another mental atmosphere to the rest of the book. Mrs Charles Smith wanted her own way, and it took all Madame Audé's tact and kindness to work out an harmonious result. In the following year Madame Duchesne managed to visit the Grand Coteau, taking with her Theresa Pratt, one of the pupils who was devotedly attached to Madame Audé. She found the little party all suffering from the climate of the Gulf of Mexico. "Madame Eugénie looks very delicate, and so does Sister Mary Layton (an American novice who had offered herself as a lay Sister). Madame Xavier has a sort of nervous fever, and Madame Gerard looks as if a breath would knock her down." But there was their appointed place, and there they stayed. As for Madame Duchesne, she nearly lost her life from yellow fever on the way back. It was in that fatal year of 1822, when the pestilence swept up the sea coast from South America as far north as Vera Cruz, in Mexico, and then passed up the seaboard states to Philadelphia. At Vera Cruz two young Englishmen, whose short story I have told in another place, died in harbour.

The history of the ten years between 1820 and 1830 must be read in the book itself. Little by little the names of new workers appear on the scene. A few were sent over by Madame Barat from France, where the order was taking extraordinary extension. Every now and then the stirring tales of the American mission fired the heart of a nun in some one of the French houses, who implored the Mother-General for leave to go over to Madame Duchesne. But more precious to the wonderful old woman were the American vocations, which began to make themselves known. Mary Layton's was the first, and she offered herself as a lay Sister in the midst of the first horrible discomfort at Fleurissant. She was twenty years of age. She took to the cows, and had one day to cut the milk with a knife and a hammer as if it had been sugar. A few months later, a French girl, Mademoiselle Eulalie St Cyr, and another with the English name of Summer, took the veil; and in May 1821 came another young girl who was destined to play a great and consoling part in Mother Duchesne's last years. Eulalie Hamilton took the name of Regis, after St Francis Regis, and lived to a great age;—was indeed still living when Mother Duchesne's life was written. Also her sister, Mathilda Hamilton, soon took the same step. The two sisters had been pupils at Fleurissant.

These new vocations had not made matters much easier for the older nuns, but they enabled new foundations to be made gradually, and Madame Barat was encouraged to supplement them by three more missionary Sisters from Paris. "The Sacred Heart was taking root in Louisiana, and there was now no fear that extension would endanger its future."

Meanwhile the Bishop was as active and determined as Madame Duchesne. A number of Flemish Jesuits had come over to America to avoid troubles in the Netherlands, and Monsignor Dubourg asked them to settle in his diocese. Two of them were priests and professed Fathers, and there were five novices still undergoing the long years of training incumbent on all who seek to join the Society. "Seven young men, full of talent, and of the spirit of St Francis Xavier, very forward in their studies, varying in age from twenty-two to twenty-seven, with their two excellent masters and some excellent lay-brothers; this is," Monsignor Dubourg wrote, "what Providence has at last sent me in answer to my prayers. If I had been allowed to choose, I could not have made a better selection."

These seven came to Fleurissant, walking and begging their way for 400 miles, from Georgetown; and their residence was that farm belonging to the Bishop, where the nuns had at first encamped. They had neither money, clothing, nor food, and fell helplessly on the tender mercies of Madame Duchesne, who had just begun to turn the corner of her own troubles. She shared her house linen and her provisions with them, and when somebody sent her fifty piastres (about £10), she despatched it at once to the young priests, who slept upon skins, and lived upon Indian corn and dripping.

These seven Jesuits became most efficient missionary priests, their labours spreading over Louisiana, and the Order of the Sacred Heart went on side by side.

Space fails to tell of the new houses opened for schools in fresh places; while Philippine Duchesne grew older and approached her seventieth year. Madame Audé left the Grand Coteau to Madame Murphy, an Irish nun sent from Paris, and herself opened a new Convent at New Orleans. There were now six houses along that 1300 miles of river, for there was one at St Louis also, built in a lonely suburb close to the forest, which soon became the centre of the town.

And now Madame Barat began to be anxious about the administration of so many houses, and their ever-increasing spheres of work.

She urged Madame Duchesne to call a provincial Council and to rule it; but the latter shrank from the task. She was essentially "soldier and missionary," and not by nature a constitutional ruler. She tried to persuade Madame Barat to "consent to whatever the Mothers of Louisiana will regulate among themselves. As to me I am only a worn-out staff, good for nothing but to be thrown away. I look at myself as an old lion without any strength to act, and that everything overwhelms and irritates." This is surely a most touching confession, and it was to a certain extent true. But Madame Barat would let no one supersede her Philippine—her "old child"—and she wrote to Madame Eugénie Audé, who was now the most capable and successful of all the heads of Houses:—"She has a right to it (the superiorship) as your senior, and the one to whom God originally trusted this mission. And, moreover, she has both virtue and experience." I should add that there is not the slightest trace of anything like human jealousy in the various letters; but Madame Audé was devoted to Madame Barat, was (with less genius) a most efficient worker, and might well have wished to take her orders direct. And we find a few pathetic words in a letter to the "old child" from Madame Barat herself, *apropos* of a reference to St Marie-d'en-Haut:—

MADAME DUCHESNE

"What remembrances you wake up in me. What happy moments we spent on that quiet, solitary mountain of yours. Times are indeed changed. For my part I live in the midst of a turmoil of business and dignities, which I try to escape from as much as I can. Often as a rest to my mind I think of and envy your wide forests and the banks of the Mississippi. Shall I ever behold them?"

No! she never did behold them. The two women spread broadcast over France and the United States the living love for Jesus Christ; they themselves never met again. When Sophie Barat wrote those lines in 1828 she was close on fifty, and Philippine ten years older. The house in Paris had gradually become the centre of aristocratic education. It had seized on the imagination of the French nobility, and to it they sent their young daughters; and the same thing occurred with the offshoots. Philippine Duchesne at sixty found herself involved in a constant struggle with the changing ideas and ideals of a vigorous new country. She tried to keep the schools attached to evangelical poverty; but American parents desired for their children the best they could get. It seemed, in 1831, that a change of direction was really inevitable. "Still Madame Barat hesitated, and dreaded taking a step which she was told was necessary. Her keen spiritual perception made her feel that, after all, the unskilfulness of saints is better than the skilfulness of others." She wrote to her friend with the quiet serenity which ever distinguished her own pen and speech, and her old friend replied peacably: "My taste for what is mean will make me think every position happy as long as I am not idle. And even if that is to be my lot, I also think that God's grace would enable me to bear it. I am quite certain that I have not a talent for governing, and I have prayed earnestly for some time past for the arrival of one who will establish regularity, and at the same time win the hearts of those under her rule." Then they consulted the Bishop, and the Bishop answered Madame Barat with decision, giving a noble testimony to the Mother Provincial. He says: "In the first place, I do not think that any of your religious would inspire the same amount of confidence as Mother Duchesne deservedly enjoys in this country. All who know her respect and venerate her virtues, which, together with her advanced age, and the experience she has acquired by her long residence in this country, have given her a great influence." And the Bishop ends his letter with these words: "The Sister whom you would place in her position would never be able to supply for her absence. Let us, then, follow the leadings of Providence. It will not fail to assist us."

So the "Old Lion" was kept at her post until the year 1834, when she was sixty-five years old. Many things happened in these years. Yellow fever again raging, fell upon the House of St Michel at New Orleans; and Mother Audé went from bed to bed, among the dying and the dead. There were two hundred persons in the house, including the nuns and children; five of the nuns died. And at St Louis, Mother Octavie Berthold, the bright, and unusually beautiful young woman who had accompanied Mother Duchesne to America, died after much suffering in 1831. The months of that illness turned Mother Duchesne's hair quite white.

At last, on the 11th of October 1834, Madame Duchesne received a letter from Madame Barat, yielding to her pressing desire, and appointing another nun, Madame Thiôfry, Superior at St Louis, and authorising her old friend to retire to Fleurissant. On the 12th the "change took place as quickly as if one cell had been exchanged for another." Madame Barat's letter was handed to the Bishop, and Madame Duchesne left that day. The same carriage which took him back to his palace—if palace it could be called—came back for her, and took her on to Fleurissant. But, says her biographer, writing many years later:—

"Mother Duchesne has never been forgotten at St Louis; often on the 1st of May, the Feast of the Apostle Philip, some of the former pupils of the Sacred Heart bring flowers for the altar, in memory of their Mother Philippine. The remembrance of her teaching still lives amongst them, and it is admitted at St Louis that the most pious, most edifying, and best informed ladies in that city are those who were educated in Mother Duchesne's school."

Chapter II

WITH THE INDIANS AT LAST

We come now to the last years of the life of Madame Duchesne — years in which, strange to relate, she was able to realise her lifelong hope of a mission to those whom she called her "dear savages," who, in this case, were, of course, the more settled tribes of Red Indians. In 1841 Madame Duchesne was an old woman past seventy. She was no longer Superior in any convent of the many she had founded, and she might well have been supposed to be past work; but the desire of her soul was as fresh as ever. A few years earlier, a very sad fate had befallen one of the tribes. It is described as a "Christian tribe," and had been brought into the Catholic Church by former missionaries, supplemented by the labours of a young priest, Father Petit, and it was he who more particularly drew the attention of the Bishop and the Jesuit Fathers to these people, called the Potowatomies. They numbered some hundreds, and were "one of these numerous families of Red Indians, originally natives of Asia, who, coming from the Behring Straits, and from the Aleutian Islands, had passed through America and peopled it at a remote and ancient period." They appear to have been evangelised in the seventeenth and eighteenth centuries by the missionaries of what they called the *Great Prayer*, and, in spite of the ever-increasing tide of emigration, they retained possession of the forests of their ancestors. But in 1835 the Congress of the United States determined to form a new state or territory, which should be exclusively Indian, into which the remains of the ancient tribes were to be gathered together under the supervision of the Government, and towards the end of 1836 these unfortunate people were driven out from their settlements, with a band of others drawn from smaller tribes. The Abbé Petit was a Breton, who had begun life as a barrister at Rennes, and then had prepared for the priesthood at St Sulpice. The savages said of him, "He is not a foreign black robe, he is a red-skin—one of ourselves"; and the affection was mutual, for the missionary wrote, "I truly love them." When M. Petit was doomed to witness their ruin, he obtained leave from his Bishop to follow them into exile. With tears and sobs, they left their little church in Indiana. "Treated like prisoners, surrounded by troops, who drove them on with their bayonets across the desert plains, these harmless Indians departed, but their priest cheered them on their sad journey." "The General to whom the direction of this brutal expedition was given, said of the young missionary, 'That man has much more power than I have.' On the 15th of November 1838, after a journey of about five hundred miles, worn out with fatigue and sickness, and decimated in numbers, the tribe reached the river of the Osages, about sixty miles from Westport, the village at the farthest point of the State of Missouri." There M. Petit was met by a Jesuit Father, who was awaiting his arrival, and had made ready to receive the poor wandering flock in the mission. "It was time for the young priest to reach the end of his journey. He was exhausted by fatigue, covered with sores, suffering from jaundice, and in a critical state. He had only strength to get to St Louis and to drag his way to the house of the Jesuit Fathers, and there he died on the 10th of February 1839, in the peace of the Lord, offering up his death for his dear Indians."

When Mother Duchesne heard this story, she wrote to France in great anxiety for permission to do something for the tribe for whom the young priest had died, and an answer came from Monsignor Rosati, "The example you made in leaving Europe for the object of making the first establishment of the Sacred Heart in America is still powerful enough to induce many others to follow it. Thank God it is so! I am indeed surprised to hear you are now asking to leave the State of Missouri to go to the savages, but those who love God never say 'It is enough.' If I did not know you I should say it was too much; but I do know you, and so I say, Go, follow your own inspirations, or, rather, the voice of God: He will be with you. I beg of Him to bless you." So Mother Duchesne, at seventy-two, set about the work. She had no money, and for the moment she had no young nuns to send on such a mission; but she said, writing about it to one of the missionaries, that if the necessary funds and workers could be got together, she herself would go and be a supernumerary, helping in the house and working so as to supply the place of some novice who would otherwise have been sent unprofessed, and who could thus remain and finish her novitiate; for, of course, they wanted fully-professed Sisters as soon as they could be got.

A missionary priest, Father de Smet, went forth and begged for the work, and five hundred piastres were collected towards the first expenses, and then came a message from Rome. Pope Gregory XVI. had sent a message to Madame Barat, in France, to say how happy he should be to hear that the Nuns of the Sacred Heart were at last going to establish themselves among the Indians. The end of it was that a little community was got together. Madame Mathevon was taken from St Charles, where she was at the time Superior, and the Indian Mission was placed under her charge. With her went Madame O'Connor, an Irish nun, who could speak both English and French, and who had been already employed in teaching the Indian women at the school of St Charles; also a Canadian Sister, Louise Amyot; and a negro called Edmund, an industrious and handy man, volunteered to help the Mission. "When people tried to alarm them about the poverty of the country, Madame Duchesne declared they could live upon milk." But it seemed to those about her that work and anxiety had even then almost brought her wonderful life to an end. The doctor said that she was in constant danger of death, and her departure on a long journey in that state was considered extremely foolish by the wise people of the vicinity. Nevertheless, the priest who was to be at the head of the travelling party insisted upon it that Mother Duchesne was not to be refused as a volunteer. "If she cannot work," he said, "she will forward the success of the Mission by her prayers." The various houses of the Sacred Heart in America sent presents of money or of linen. The Bishop of Natchez came to St Louis on the eve of the departure of the colony, and gave it his blessing. About twenty gentlemen and ladies accompanied the nuns to the boat, and a sum of fifty piastres was added that day to their little fund. It was on the 29th of June, the Feast of the Apostles St Peter and St Paul. And so they steamed off on the calm waters of the Missouri River, and Madame Duchesne walked up and down the deck as if she were young again. They landed at Westport, and had still, as was supposed, two days of travelling by land. The only carriage to be had was a wretched car, which jolted the venerable old Mother, and gave her dreadful pain. The two days' travelling were prolonged to eight, and they were often hindered and pursued on their way by the inhabitants of towns and villages, who entreated them to stay and open schools for the education of their daughters. Madame Mathevon relates that when they were still eighteen miles distant from the Indian Settlement they were met by "two savages," who began by kneeling down at the feet of the priest and asking for his blessing, and they told him that on the preceding evening the whole of the tribe had assembled and awaited till nightfall the arrival of the women of the Great Spirit, but they had not appeared. "Go and tell them," the Father said, "that to-morrow, by the first light of the sun, we shall be with them."

The most extraordinary account is given of the way in which they were received. A hundred and fifty Indians met them on horseback, with white flags, and their heads dressed with many-coloured plumes. When the procession halted at the Curé's house, the four nuns and the five Jesuit Fathers were invited to alight and take seats on some benches, the "savages" standing in four lines on each side of them. Father Verhaegen, who had escorted the Sisters, began by presenting Madame Duchesne, although she was not the Superior. "My children," he said, "here is a lady who, for thirty-five years, has been asking God to let her come to you," upon which the chief of the tribe addressed her a compliment. His wife then did the same, with these words, "To show you our joy, all the women of the tribe, married and unmarried, will now embrace you." The nuns went bravely through the ceremony, and then had to shake hands with the men, who, with their chief at their head, filed before them, every one of whom insisted on giving his greeting. "These marks of welcome were repeated seven hundred times. Madame Duchesne, in spite of excessive fatigue, gladly went through it." The name of this village was Sugar Creek.

Although this settlement had been Christianised,

Mother Duchesne was pained to see the faithful devour seven meals a day, and do nothing for the rest of their time, but they were peaceable and good, while some of the neighbouring tribes were said to be actually cannibals.

The nuns soon managed to open a school for fifty young girls. The children were extremely handy with their fingers; the women also came to learn to work. The Jesuit Fathers taught the men to farm, and the nuns of the Sacred Heart taught the women to cook, to sew, to spin, and to weave, and how to make themselves clothes. "Since they had been Christians, their dress simply consisted of two yards of blue cloth wound round their body, and the men went to church in long shirts. The Sisters could hardly keep their countenances at first, when they saw these good people going up solemnly to Holy Communion in such strange attire, and to recover their gravity they had to think of the white robes the Neophytes wore in the early days of the Church." In this new scene new life seemed to come to Madame Duchesne. She wrote to her own sister, "My health has much improved here; I have gained strength; my sight is clearer, and in spite of my seventy-three years, I enjoy the use of all my faculties"; and she wrote to the Mother-General in Paris, "I feel when I hear of the Rocky Mountains or other missions of that sort, the same longing desire I had in France to come to America, and in America to be sent to the savages. They tell me that people live to a hundred in the Rocky Mountains. Now that I am quite well again, and being after all, only seventy-three, why should I not have ten more years of work before me; then at other times it seems to me more perfect to await the events which will decide my fate." She could not, however, learn the Indian language. "It is too barbarous and too difficult," she wrote to her sister, "six or eight, or ten syllables, and no dictionary, no grammar, no books. I shall never be able to master such a language"; so instead she devoted herself to prayer. "The dear, good mother prays all day," said Madame Mathevon, "for now she can do nothing else." Four hours in the morning, and as many in the evening she spent in the little chapel, which was the parish church. There she took up her abode.

"The savages when they saw her kneeling motionless before the tabernacle, were seized with a holy veneration, and used to come up silently behind her and kiss the hem of her worn-out habit. According to their custom of designating people by their characteristics, they called her "the woman who prays always." In the evening she would take a walk on the prairie and remind herself of her dear Grenoble by singing the old French hymns sung by the inhabitants of her mountain convent. The Indians came to look upon her "as a supernatural creature, and paid her a sort of worship, bringing her their best fruits and freshest eggs, as they used formerly to their Manitou."

But the climate of Sugar Creek was too cold for the dear old woman. The winter proved peculiarly severe, the food ran short, and maize and sweet potatoes were for a time the only sustenance of the nuns. Such a diet as this was very bad for a person as weak as Madame Duchesne now was. The Superior wrote on the 5th of February 1842, "She is much aged and often very ill. The life here is too hard for a person of her advanced age." In March Mother Galitzin came to Sugar Creek. She was the Assistant-General in America, and it had only been out of obedience to Mother Barat in Paris that she had consented to send the venerable Mother Duchesne to this northern mission; and now, in spite of her courage, it became evidently impossible for the aged nun to stay there. Dr Kenrick, coadjutor of the Bishop of St Louis, came in June, and was of the same opinion. She looked very ill, and he feared that if allowed to remain she would die. She begged hard to be allowed to stay; she wanted to die and be buried amongst her Indians, but she resigned herself to her fate, and wrote, "God knows the reasons of this recall, and that is enough." And so in July 1842, Madame Duchesne again embarked on the Missouri River to return to the Convent of St Charles. She was escorted by the Superior of the Jesuits, Father Verhaegen; she had remained with her Indians just a year. In one of her letters, she says, "I feel as if I were taken out of my element, now that I have left the country of the savages, and that I can now only languish for our one great home whence we shall never depart."

MADAME DUCHESNE

The Indian Settlements were eventually sacrificed to the policy of the Government of the United States. "For three hundred years the Catholic Church had struggled by her charity, her courage, and her devotion, to save the Red Indian tribes from wholesale destruction. It is an honour to the Society of the Sacred Heart to have worked in the cause, to have been the bearer to an oppressed race of the merciful invitations of Jesus Christ to all who suffer and are heavily burdened, and most honourable will it ever be to Madame Duchesne that she opened to her Sisters the road to this *Apostolate*; after which she had so long sighed." But alas! it is an American writer who has said, "If heathenism has disappeared in America, it is because the heathens have almost disappeared." And it is surely sad to have to say that Hiawatha is no more.

Chapter III

THE LAST TEN YEARS

Mother Duchesne lived on ten years after her return from Sugar Creek to St Charles. She was eighty-three when she died in that far-off American home —the Frenchwoman from Grenoble, who had worked in the prisons of 1793, surviving the First Empire, the Restoration, the overthrow of the Orleans Dynasty, the election of Louis Napoleon as President of France, and the *coup d'état*. Her return was hailed as a blessing by the community at St Charles, but there is something very pathetic about the story of these last years. She had one great grief, the closing of the house at Fleurissant, where the American novitiate had begun. It was her singular fate never to be herself able to plan a permanent thing in a permanent place, while the spiritual efficacy of her devoted life spread in all directions. In 1844 one of her oldest nuns, Catherine Lamarre, who had come with her from France, died at Fleurissant just before its suppression. Even the convent of St Marie-d'en-Haut, close to Grenoble, was eventually parted with to the Ursulines. Mother Audé, who had worked with her through those first American years, had been recalled to Paris, and Madame Barat, her dearest friend, the aged nun was destined never to see again.

MADAME DUCHESNE

Her biographer says that if there was in Mother Duchesne's heart a more tender and more delicate chord than any other, it was beyond question the tie of friendship and religion which bound her to Mother Barat, and herewith again, she passed through an experience of unaccountable suffering. The circumstances are carefully veiled, but we are told that the letters passing between the two old friends, one of whom was the foundress of the whole order, and the other the foundress of the American Mission, were totally suppressed for two whole years. The biographer hopes that this suppression did not arise from any malicious intention, but it is, in any case, a melancholy revelation of human nature. When the facts were cleared up, Mother Duchesne thus described to her revered friend the anguish she had endured:—" I had the painful conviction that you had lost all affection for me, and though I thought it must be through my own fault, this did not prevent my heart from being withered by grief." The story reads as if the cause of the supposed estrangement would never have been discovered, but that, about that time, 1847, the Mother-General in Paris got so anxious about her dear old Philippine, that she sent Madame Amelie Jouve to assume the government of a house in Canada, and ordered her to go first to St Charles, though it was some hundreds of leagues out of the way. This nun was, of course, daughter to Madame Jouve, the beloved sister of Madame Duchesne, to whom the traveller brought " light and joy and a sort of resurrection of the heart." Madame Amelie Jouve wrote to Madame Barat as soon as she had arrived at St Charles. The letter is dated the 14th of September 1847: "This letter will apprise you that I am with my holy aunt. I can say like St Antony, 'I have seen St Paul in the Desert.' Yes; I have seen a great saint who is drawing near to the end of her life. I found her very feeble, and her voice so weak that it is sometimes difficult to make out what she says. She received me as if I had been an angel sent from heaven. This noble soul, whose lot it has always been to have great crosses to bear, suffered terribly from the thought that she had displeased our Mothers, and particularly our Mother-General. A perfect expression of joy appeared in her face when she read our reverend Mother's letter and heard that she had sent me to St Charles on purpose to see her. Our days are spent in conversation, in which the names of our Mothers and Sisters in France incessantly occur, and also reminiscences of the early days of the Society."

And Madame Duchesne wrote, wonderfully comforted, to Madame Barat, and to her sister, Madame Jouve, to whom she said :—" It would be impossible to describe to you all the pleasure Amelie's visit has given me. It was more than thirty years since I had seen her, and what merit she has acquired since that time! She has given me the most interesting details about our numerous family, many of whom I have never known, but whom I often recommend in prayer to our Lord Jesus Christ. I admire, dearest sister, the sacrifice you made in parting with a daughter whom I have now had the happiness of knowing. Our Sisters of St Charles were delighted to see her, and would have much wished to keep her here, and it was the same at the House of St Louis." From that time forward, Madame Barat kept constantly writing and sending presents to Mother Philippine. She tells her "dear Mother, and old child of mine," that she is always present to her mind when praying to our Lord. "I think of you and speak of you often, especially to our young Sisters, when I want to excite in them zeal for souls and generosity in sacrificing everything for the love of Jesus," and again Madame Barat writes, " How long it is since I have heard from you. I long to do so. Write to me in a detailed manner everything you do"; and in a postscript she adds, "If there is anything you want, my dear friend, tell me," and without waiting to be asked she despatched anything she thought would please her; but it was not easy to send presents to Madame Duchesne, who would wear nothing but old clothes, and would never admit that she had any want in the world. However, she was obliged to answer Madame Amelie Jouve when she quoted the orders of the Mother-General, and inquired " what there was that she could do to please the servant of God?" Then the old nun answered that she had only two wishes in the world, one was to recover possession of the picture of St Francis Regis, which was taken away when the altar at Fleurissant was demolished; and the other wish was that she should end her days under the government of her daughter, Mother Regis. This latter nun, called by the outward world Madame Hamilton, was, therefore, named Superior at St Charles. She had been the first American novice. So delighted was Madame Duchesne at the fulfilment of this request that she writes, "For some time past my memory and my strength have been rapidly diminishing: this year I feel much better, and I am afraid it will be still some time before I arrive at my eternal home. I ascribe this improvement to the gift you have made us of our Mother Hamilton. Everything is now at peace in this house." And Mother Hamilton, on her side, was just as grateful for the privilege of ministering during her last days to the woman who had brought her into the Society of the Sacred Heart. She writes that she was sleeping in Madame Duchesne's room, making her bed, and helping her to rise in the morning. "Every care I possibly can I take of her, though not always as much as I should wish, for she still thinks that she must do penance, and that everything is too good for her, so we quarrel now and then, and sometimes I get my way, and sometimes she gets hers." In these last years Madame Duchesne could do nothing but pray. Her biographer describes her as "a woman of desires—a Moses on the mountain"—"forever lifting up her hands and her heart in prayer, and imploring victory and salvation for the people of God." She prayed constantly and especially for the thousands of children in the schools which she had helped to found. She did not particularly like the style of modern education for girls. She had a suspicion regarding algebra and astronomy. Her conception of the best character in women was based upon her own intimate knowledge of that sturdy, loving heart of the working Frenchwoman, of which she herself was so great an example in her own original rank of life, and Madame Barat in another. And after her prayers for the children came those for the mission and the missionaries. She prayed constantly for her Indians, whom she regarded as innocent, and for the sinners in the States who swore, and drank, and worked on Sunday. When fire and pestilence fell upon St Louis, thousands of its inhabitants died. In some houses only the children were left alive. But Madame Duchesne sat upon her mountain and lifted her hands and her heart in prayer. In 1852, she gradually failed away. She wrote to Madame Barat: " My old age is spent sadly enough; my eyesight is weak, but God is always good. It is a consolation to be silently occupied near the Great Tabernacle." In another letter, she says: " I do not know, my dear, good, venerable Mother, if you will be able to read my handwriting. I am so old, but still about, thanks be to God who admits me to His table almost every day." The people about her, like the savages, became gradually convinced of her extraordinary sanctity. During her prayers the children often noticed rays of light about her head. They used to look at her when she was before the Tabernacle, and to whisper to one another, " Mother Duchesne is praying," and to watch for the moment when she came out of church in order to curtsey respectfully to her. And an old man of eighty, who was employed in the house, was one day seen gesticulating and talking to himself. A Sister asked him what was the matter, and he said, "I have seen something I have never seen before; Mother Duchesne is a saint," and then he explained that at the moment when she received Holy Communion her face shone with a bright light. In the autumn of 1852 she said that she was conscious of increasing failure of mind and memory; but there is no trace that anybody else perceived this. "I did not expect that I should lose my mind," she used sorrowfully to say, "but God has willed to humble my pride." Her confessor told her to leave off "mental application," but it is certain that the "peculiar trial which she had apprehended was mercifully spared her, as her reason retained to the end its clearness, and her character its energy." She passed away on the 18th of October 1852, in the eighty-fourth year of her age, the forty-seventh of her religious profession, and the thirty-fourth of her residence in America. She had said, "When I am dead, everything will progress," and the schools of the Sacred Heart, which had taken root in all directions during the last ten years of prayer, took a still greater extension in succeeding years, as if she were then, elsewhere, pleading for them with still greater efficacy. They extended their sphere all over the American States. They are now on the two sides of the Isthmus of Panama, and upon the Isles; they are in South America and in Canada. In 1879 there were twelve hundred nuns working in America in thirty-one educational convents, with three thousand pupils of the upper class of girls, and four thousand five hundred children, all receiving a Christian education. In their present schools and orphanages the numbers can be easily ascertained. It is eighty years ago this very year since Mother Duchesne landed at New Orleans, on the 25th of May, to fulfil a purpose which she had already cherished for more than half a lifetime. Some there were who grieved that she was never recalled to her native France, but results such as those of Philippine Duchesne's career can only be achieved by a total sacrifice of self; and although for five-and-thirty years she did not see the beloved face of Madame Barat, in twelve more years the two old friends and fellow-workers were again united, when Madame Barat died in 1865.

MOTHER SETON OF EMMETTSBURG

For the three lives whose portraits reduced in miniature have preceded the one which is placed at the head of this page, there have been ample materials accumulated. Two of those lives were prolonged into old age; the third was comparatively shortened, but the immense extension of Mrs M'Aulay's work has caused records to pour in from far distant places, and has made the task of speaking of her much easier. But the curtailed record of Mrs Seton's few working years (she died at forty-seven) leaves a wondering admiration of the intensity of a nature which left so deep an impress on the country of her birth, and all the more so because no attempt to give a connected biography appears to have been made until thirty-one years after her death. A diary kept of her painful sojourn with her dying husband in the quarantine of Leghorn did get printed by the indiscretion of some private person four years before her death, and the editor makes the strange observation that: "Although the author is now buried within the dark walls of a monastery, it is to be hoped all her writings may emerge to the light, for they will be considered an acquisition to the Christian library, and precious in the annals of American literature, and may vie with those of Miss Smith, More, and others in celebrity."

But Mrs Seton did not in the least resemble the once famous and learned Elizabeth Smith or Hannah More. She never aspired to teach anybody by her pen, and never regarded herself in any way as an apostle. Her private letters seem to have been the only documents she left behind her. Though controversy raged round her, and her becoming a Catholic was the cause of deep indignation to an influential group of relatives and friends, there is no trace of her making either appeal or reply. She pursued her difficult way quietly, if often with an aching heart; and has left a name which will never be effaced from the religious history of the United States; the " dark walls of the monastery" had very wide windows and a very large door. There are lights in all those windows and the portal is never shut.

Elisa Ann Bayley was born, a British subject, in New York in 1774. She was the younger daughter of Dr Richard Bayley by his first marriage with Catherine Charlton, but her mother died before she was three years old. That mother was daughter to an Episcopalian clergyman, and an uncle, Dr Charlton, was a much respected physician, while Dr Richard Bayley was extremely eminent. In Colonial America this family counted with the best, and Dr Bayley was a man whom we must regard as on a level with the Edgworths and Darwins of a hundred years ago. Like them he gave his daughter an excellent education under his own close personal superintendence, and like them he belonged to the school of eighteenth-century philosophy. Before his daughter's birth he had gone over to London to avail himself of advantages not to be procured in America, and wrote home : " The anatomist, Dr Hunter, gives me great encouragement, and thinks that by applying myself closely to anatomy and the operative part of surgery this winter (1770) I may with ease qualify myself for a practitioner in surgery in any part of the world." On his return to New York, he presumably obtained the desired qualification, as he "commenced practice in connection with Dr Charlton, his brother-in-law." His daughter, as she grew up, adored him, and in considering Mrs Seton's later career, we must do justice to the noble stock from which she came. It is told how Dr Bayley became a most successful operator, and how he combated yellow fever, which at that time was not restrained within Southern limits. In 1799 he published a work on the pestilence :—a work "purely practical" the fruit of "a painful and hazardous experience in the disease." In the end his life was sacrificed to his charity. He had been made Health Physician to the port of New York, and he accordingly passed much of his time at Staten Island, where vessels were detained in quarantine. "Here scenes of distress and suffering which occurred among emigrants who frequently arrived in considerable numbers, and which almost defied description, called into constant action the energetic benevolence of Dr Bayley, while the yellow fever was raging on board the infected vessels, hurrying to the grave hundreds of unfortunate beings who had scarcely seen the light of day since they had embarked from home, and little infants were dying by scores since admitted into the fresh air, or famishing at the mother's breast, unable to receive other nourishment or to find it. Dr Bayley was everywhere seen among the sick and the dying—sometimes carrying almost lifeless babes in his own arms to place them in comfortable beds; to the countless numbers that came from foreign countries, and were suffering from the pestilence, he was a real father. In offices of humanity he never wearied, and every rising sun found him already two or three hours engaged in the work of charity." At this time his daughter "Bett," as he fondly called her, was already married and a mother, and he would not allow her to render him any assistance in labours which might have compromised her own household. We note that even then her imagination was struck by the piety of the Irish emigrants. The first thing these poor people did when they got their tents on Staten Island, was to assemble on the grass and, kneeling, offer public thanks to God.

The period had arrived when Mrs Seton was to experience the first of her many bitter sorrows. She had from infancy loved her one remaining parent with a passionate ardour natural to her temperament. Her letters to "Mr Papa," and his to his "little Bett" are wonderfully pretty. In one of them, dated in the year 1800, she writes to him: "My father, a little faithful heart has been present with you this hour past, and I have engaged to copy from it . . . that it regrets your absence, is extremely anxious for your present safety, and will rejoice when you return"; and a week later: "The heart of your Betty jumped for joy at the sight of the letter that was to tell her of your safe arrival, that you were well, and in the midst of friends, and can it be that there is any charm in your visit to Albany to compensate for your absence from New York. . . I have been copying so many English letters, French letters, etc., that one eye is bound, the other shut; therefore, Mr Papa, I wish you a night of rest and myself the same, your most dear daughter, E. A. Seton." She was only twenty-seven when she lost this dear father, whose life was sacrificed to his duty in the following manner: It was in the very hot weather of an American August, in the year 1801, that Dr Bayley "directed the passengers and crew of an Irish emigrants' vessel, struck with yellow fever, to come on shore to the rooms and tents appointed for them, leaving their luggage behind. This was in the evening. Early the following morning, upon going to the hospital, he found that his orders had been disobeyed, and crew and passengers, men, women, and children, well, sick, and dying, with all their baggage, were huddled together in one apartment, where they had passed the night. Into this apartment, before it had been ventilated, he imprudently entered, and remained but a moment, being compelled to retire by the most deadly sickness at the stomach, and an intense pain at the head which seized him immediately upon entering the room. Returning home, he retired to his bed, from which he never rose." Mrs Seton watched him continually. She was at that time an ardent Episcopalian, and most anxious for the welfare of his soul. "She knew that his religious ideas were too conformable to the then prevalent philosophy, and she feared, notwithstanding his great moral virtues, lest his salvation might be in danger," and it is recorded that in the anguish of his deathbed she went to the cradle where her infant child was sleeping, clasped it in her arms, and going out on the piazza of the building, she there raised the little innocent babe towards heaven, and appealed to the divine compassion, saying, "O Jesus, my merciful Father and God, take this little innocent offering; I give it to Thee with all my heart, but save my father's soul." The offering was not accepted; the little child lived for many years, and on the seventh day of his sickness Dr Bayley expired, leaving behind him a great reputation as an efficient physician, "a man of strong character, inflexible in his attachments, invincible in his dislikes, and unbrooking of insults. In temper fiery, yet suddenly cool—a fault which he knew and regretted—thoroughly fearless, somewhat too strongly partial to certain patients, but withal charitable to a fault." This account of him is taken from Thacker's "American Medical Biography," which also gives an anecdote of his disinterested kindness: "A physician of Staten Island, having a case which required a difficult operation, requested

Dr Bayley to perform it, but he declined on account of the distance and the large practice which demanded his attention. The applicant, in pressing his request, at length observed to him, 'It is true, Doctor, they are not able to pay you much, for they are poor.' 'Poor, are they?' said Dr Bayley. 'Come, I will go with you,' and true to his word he went, and performed the operation with the utmost care and success."

There is no sign in Mrs Seton's letters or papers that she in the future tormented herself in regard to this dear father's soul.

We now come to a grievous experience which was to test to the utmost Mrs Seton's resolution and submission. In the spring of 1803 her husband's health, which had always been extremely delicate, was seen to be rapidly declining, and he was advised to try the experiment of a sea voyage, in the hope that it might save him. Eliza Bayley had married him at the age of twenty; she was now twenty-nine, and had five children, two boys and three girls. The Setons appear to have been quite equal in social rank to her own family, and they also were attached to the English interest. Her husband, William Seton, was a merchant, and commercial intercourse had made him long and favourably known to the Messrs Filiechi, wealthy merchants of Leghorn. William Seton had visited Italy in his early youth, and in 1803 he was thirty-seven years old. The plan of travel seemed to the married pair perfectly reasonable, and Mrs Seton prepared to accompany the beloved invalid, leaving her younger children to her near relatives, and taking with her the eldest daughter, Anna Maria, then in her ninth year. Before starting, she wrote to one of her dearest friends: "My dear, dear Eliza, your tenderness and affection calls me back, for often, often, with all I have to do, I forget I am here. The cloud that overpowers me can only be borne by striving to get above it. Seton has had new and severe suffering since I saw you. All say it is presumption and next to madness to undertake our voyage, but you know we reason differently. Saturday is now the day. Everything is ready and on board." She then utters some strong expressions of religious faith, adding, "My heart trembles within me, and I can only say, Take my darlings in your arms, and do not let the remembrance of anything I have ever done that has vexed you come twice to your thoughts. I know it will not, but it seems to me like my last hour with all that I love." The voyage seemed to revive the invalid, and the precious life of the husband and father might possibly have been much prolonged but for the disastrous experience which met the travellers at Leghorn. It reads like a bad dream of the Middle Ages. A French ship had brought the news of yellow fever in New York, and the American vessel was banished into the Roads, and the poor invalid was sent off with his baggage to the Lazaretto River. Of course his wife and child accompanied him. The place was some miles out of Leghorn, and they found themselves placed in a large house,

and in a room up twenty stone steps, a room with
high arched ceiling, brick floor, and naked walls.
The capitano, who had accompanied them, sent
in three warm eggs, a bottle of wine, and some
slices of bread. Mr Seton's mattress was soon
spread, and he was placed upon it, but he could
not touch wine nor eggs, and all the little niceties
of food which had supported him during the voyage
were absolutely deficient. Mrs Seton was told to
look up to the window of the capitano's neighbouring house, in which sat Mrs Philip Filiechi, who
spoke to them most affectionately, and sent out
chairs to them, but she could not come down and
touch them; and the chairs, once used by the
travellers, could not return to the capitano's house.
There was no fire in their room, and poor little
Anna got hold of the rope that had tied her box,
and began skipping to warm herself, " for the cold
walls and bricks made us shiver" (they had reached
Italy in October). Then at sunset dinner came
from the kind Filiechis, with other necessaries, and
poor Mrs Seton went up to look at her friends
through a grating. Before little Anna went to
sleep she said, " Mamma, if Papa died here—but
God will be with us," and the poor mother says in
her diary that the wind in the apartment " almost
puts out my light, and blows on my William at
every crevice, and over our chimney like loud
thunder." The next day was Sunday. " I
asked William what we should do for breakfast.
The doors were unbarred, and a bottle of milk set
down in the entrance of the room, poor Philip

fearing to come too near. Little Anna and William ate it with bread, and I walked the floor with a crust and a glass of wine. William could not sit up; his ague came on, and my soul's agony with it." Then these unfortunate people went through as much of the church service as the invalid could bear. Dinner was sent from town, and a servant, who, once admitted, stayed with them during their quarantine. His name was Louis, an old man, " very little, with grey hairs, and blue eyes which changed their expression from joy to sorrow, doing their best to console and enliven." Mrs Seton could not eat the dinner, and the little old man lifted his hands and began praying. On the Monday the capitano came with his guards and put up a very neat bed and curtains for Mr Seton, sent by Philip Filiechi. The capitano, taking off his great hat, was revealed as a grey-headed man, with a very kind face, and he said to Mrs Seton : " I had a wife—I loved her—I loved her ; she gave me a daughter, which she commended to my care, and died." He then clasped his hands, looking at the unfortunate pair, and said, " If God calls, what can we do? *et que voulez vous, signora ?*" This dreadful misery went on for a month. Louis brought them lovely flowers, jessamine, geraniums, and pinks ; and he made excellent soup, which he cooked with charcoal in a little pot. The poor woman very soon knew that nothing could save her husband, confined in this place of high and damp walls, exposed to cold and want. There was no fire except the charcoal. The Italian friends did their very best, but they could not save him. Mrs Seton writes in her diary: "Dear, dear William, I can sometimes inspire him for a few moments to feel that it would not be sad to die, but he always says, 'My Father and my God, Thy Will be done.'" One day Mrs Seton went to the railings with little Anna to receive from the capitano's daughter a baby doll she had been making for the child. The girl had a kind, good countenance, and hung on her father's arm, and Mrs Seton says "she has refused an offer of marriage that she may take care of him. Such a sight awakened my recollections." The resident chaplain of the British chapel at Leghorn, Mr Hall, came one morning, and went away, with a promise to come again, but he also must have been kept outside the grating. Little Anna read in the Gospel one day that John the Baptist was imprisoned, and said, "Yes, papa, Herod imprisoned him, and Miss Herodias gave him liberty." "No, my dear, she had him beheaded." "Well, papa, she released him from prison and sent him to God"; and the mother adds, "It is a child after my own heart." And then came December the 14th, and she writes: "Five days more and our quarantine is ended. Lodgings are engaged at Pisa, on the borders of the Arno. My heart used to be full of poetical visions about this famous river, but it has no room for visions now. One only vision is before it. No one ever saw my William without giving him the qualities of an amiable man, but to see that character exalted to the peaceful, humble Christian, waiting the will of God with a patience that seems more than human, and a firm faith which could do honour to the most distinguished piety, is a happiness that was allowed only to the poor little mother, who is separated from all other happiness connected with this condition of things." Rain and storm came almost every day. Mrs Seton wrote that the dampness would have been thought dangerous for a person in health, and she adds, " Captain, you need not always point your soul's finger there up to God; if I thought our condition the providence of man—instead of the weeping Magdalene, as you so graciously call me—you would find me a lioness, willing to pull the Lazaretto about your ears, if it was possible, that I might carry off my poor prisoner to breathe the air of heaven in some more hospitable place. To keep a poor soul, who comes to your country for his life, thirty days shut up in damp walls, smoke and wind from all quarters blowing even the curtains round his bed, and his bones almost through, and now in the shadow of death trembling if he only stands a few minutes! He is to go to Pisa for his health. This day his prospects are very far from Pisa; but, O my Heavenly Father, I know that these contradictory conditions are permitted, and guided by Thy wisdom, which only is light." And so they got on until December 19th, when, at eleven o'clock in the morning, Mr Seton was lifted into the arms of two men, and taken from the Lazaretto to Mr Filiechi's carriage, surrounded by a multitude of gazers. His wife's heart beat almost to fainting with a fear lest he should die in the exertion; but the air revived him. His spirits were cheerful, and through fifteen miles of heavy roads he was supported, and appeared stronger than when he set out. One week Mr Seton lingered on in Pisa. On Christmas Day, the sick man said he wished he could have the Sacrament, and his poor wife put a little wine in a glass, and said different parts of psalms and prayers, and gave him what she called the cup of thanksgiving, as a reminder of the Sacrament which they could not receive. On Christmas Day she seems to have spent all the hours upon her knees by his bedside, and says that she had eaten nothing, "Every moment that I could I looked upon my William." She prayed for him, and he, on his part, anxiously prayed for his release. On the 26th he spoke of his babies in America, and he said to little Anna, "Oh, if your father could take you with him," and at midnight he reached out both his arms, and said repeatedly: "You promised me you would go; come, come, fly." At four o'clock, the hard struggle ceased. Nature sank into a settled calm —"My dear wife and little ones!—and my Christ Jesus, have mercy and receive me," was all I could distinguish, and again he repeated, "My Christ Jesus," till, at a quarter-past seven on Tuesday morning the 27th, his soul was released, and his wife adds, "And mine from a struggle next to death," and Mrs Seton kneeled down, and made her little girl kneel by her side, and thank God that her father had died in hopeful peace.

On the very day of William Seton's death his wife had to leave his inanimate remains, and travel to Leghorn with her poor little daughter. The Italian laws in regard to death and interment have always been of the most rigid description. They at all times regarded consumption as highly infectious, and would strip a patient's room, not only of curtains and carpets, but even of the very wall paper. They did this years before the advance of science had produced the same conviction in the minds of physicians in England. Indeed, so strong was the general feeling in Italy, that the poor wife had to lay out her husband's corpse herself, and the people around her, gazing at her with astonishment, exclaimed that if she were not a heretic she would be a saint. The kind Filiechis now took complete possession of the widow and the orphan child, who remained with them rather more than a month, and during that month of January impressions were made upon her heart and intellect which changed the whole current of Mrs Seton's life. She herself said long afterwards, when pressed with a question as to why she had become a Catholic, that "she had seen in Italy the practical working of the Catholic Church." It was on the 3rd of April that she started on her return to America, and in the same ship which had brought her to Europe. Antonio Filiechi, the younger of the two brothers, accompanied her to the United States. "A desire to see the country and to attend to certain matters of business had long made a visit to the New World an object of interest to him, but he was decided to undertake the voyage by the opportunity now presented of becoming the protector to Mrs Seton." Philip Filiechi was also the best and truest of friends, and a half-brother of Mr Seton's appears to have been associated with them. On the 20th of April Mrs Seton was still upon the sea, and she notes in her diary, "This day thirty-seven years ago, my Seton was born—does he pass his birthday in heaven? Oh, my husband, how my soul would rejoice to be united with yours—if rejoicing before His Throne, how beautiful—if in the bonds of justice, how willingly would I share your pain to lessen it. My Saviour and my God, be not angry with me. Consider my desire and have mercy. My dear, dear little children, no feast of mirth to-day!"

"On the 20th of April we have passed the Straits and again I have seen Gibraltar, with a thousand bitter recollections that must always occur to my thoughts when I think of the sufferings of my William which we passed together. I have but passed two days which I wish to remember—one in view of the towering Alps which separate Italy from France, and also the day we were becalmed opposite the town of Valencia and surrounded by Lord Nelson's fleet. We were boarded by the Belle-Isle, and on the evening before by the 74-Excellent."

The little party were two months at sea and landed at New York on the 4th of June. Mrs Seton found the children well, but a very dear sister of her husband's on the verge of the grave, and she writes to Antonio Filiechi's wife at Leghorn that "Miss Seton's uncommon piety and innocence, and strong confidence in God" are her sole consolation.

Mrs Seton had gradually made up her mind to join the Catholic Church, and found herself in a position of very heavy trial, spiritual and temporal. It was a sad distress to her to pain her former pastor, John Hay Hobart, a noted Episcopalian clergyman in New York. Her family on both sides were, as we have already said, English in sympathy, and strong Church people in faith, and it was years before they became reconciled to her change, even if they can be said ever to have become so. But they had eventually to witness her winning the respect and affection, not only of an immense circle of private friends, but of the Government of her country. The story is a remarkable one, and shows what great results from small beginnings rise.

The first difficulty which beset the widowed mother was, of course, the question of maintenance for herself and her five children. Antonio Filiechi gave her a brother's help, and in addition to his other acts of generosity, showed a deep and efficient interest in the education of the little group. During a visit to Canada in the summer of 1805 he made inquiries about the Collegiate Establishment of Montreal, intending to place her two boys in that institution—one of whom was now seven, and the other nine years of age; but the little fellows were, after mature reflection, entered at Georgetown, a college in the United States, and Mrs Seton herself opened a boarding-house in the northern suburbs of New York." An elderly gentleman and relative, knowing that for the support of her family she was dependent on her exertions, would frequently take a basket, go himself to the market, purchase a joint of meat which he knew she liked, for he had in more prosperous days been a guest at her table, add to it some other little article, and carry it himself to her humble dwelling, fearful of entrusting so delicate a commission to a servant." In 1806 Antonio Filiechi returned to Italy. He had been the best of brothers to her, and their separation was a great grief. Her biographer says that in parting it was "a consolation of these mutually cherished friends to reflect that religion and fortitude had united them, that one had succoured the fatherless and the widow in their tribulation, while the other had found the priceless treasure of faith which would more than suffice the loss of mere earthly comforts and possessions." They never met again.

Amid the difficulties of her position she was comforted especially by the expressions of regard and friendship which were received from Bishop Carroll and the Rev. Mr Cheverus of Boston. Father Cheverus became very eminent in latter years; and, as time went on, we find her also adopted into the friendship of Father William Dubourg, then President of St Mary's College in Baltimore. He it was who, later in life, became Bishop of Louisiana, and afforded Madame Duchesne her first chance of going to America. It is interesting that the same man should have given the needed opportunity to two such women. Mrs Seton seems to have hitherto lived exclusively in New York, the city of her birth, and where all her relatives appear to have remained in excellent social positions, and it was in New York, that she met with Father Dubourg at the residence of a gentleman who was their common friend. "In the course of conversation the members mentioned some particulars respecting the prosperity of the college over which the priest presided, and the vacant lots of ground belonging to it. Mrs Seton remarked in a jesting way, 'I will come and beg.' M. Dubourg, after inquiring about her present position, said to her, 'We also wish to form a small school for the promotion of religious instruction for children whose parents are interested on that point.' Mrs Seton objected to her want of talent, to which he replied, 'We want example more than talents,' and he then told her that if she would come and help at Baltimore, her two sons would be admitted into St Mary's College without any expense," and her little daughters, of course, remain under her own wing. Some of her friends in New York were also of opinion that her removal to Baltimore was an excellent scheme, since " her principles excluded her from the confidence of the inhabitants of New York." She therefore left the city which had been the home of her childhood, and in the arrangement of the plan which now wholly engrossed the mind of M. Dubourg, he suggested the expediency of taking two red-brick houses, which had been recently built near St Mary's Seminary, and were well suited to the object contemplated. He did not want her pupils to increase with too great rapidity, saying, "The fewer you will have in the beginning, the lighter your task, and the easier it will be to establish that spirit of regularity and piety which must be the mainspring of your machinery. There are in the country enough, and perhaps too many, mixed schools in which ornamental accomplishments are the only objects of education. We have none that I know where their instruction is connected with and made subservient to pious instruction, and such a one you certainly wish yours to be." This letter is dated on the 8th of June 1808, and it is probable that Mrs Seton did not receive it until after her arrival in Baltimore, as she left New York on the 9th. Little as she knew it, that journey from New York to Baltimore was the first step in the foundation of Emmettsburg, and the planting of the Order of the Sisters of Charity in the United States.

The mother and the three little daughters travelled in a sailing packet. At this period steamboat navigation was only beginning to be introduced. Robert Fulton had made the first steam voyage in the previous year of 1807, by the River Hudson from New York to Albany. They took six days in getting to Baltimore, reaching their destination late at night on a Wednesday, the 15th of June. Mother and children slept on board, and next morning a carriage conveyed them to St Mary's Chapel, for it was the Feast of Corpus Christi. After the service she was introduced to a new circle of friends, from whom she met with a warm and cordial reception which made her feel perfectly at home. A few days later she went to Georgetown for the purpose of moving her two sons from the college of that place to the institution under the charge of Father Dubourg. Her removal to Baltimore with a view to conducting a "Family Academy" added to the interest with which she was looked upon by a large class of the community. One wealthy gentleman, a former governor of Maryland, begged her to go and live in his house, "and offered to take her children as his own," but in thanking him she "politely declined accepting the offer, with the observation that she did not leave the world for the purpose of entering it again," and she lost no time in opening her school; and she also wrote to tell Antonio Filiechi of her happy prospects, who wrote back that she must draw upon him for any money that she needed, telling her that his affairs were most prosperous; and so the good Antonio, who regarded her as a sister, helped her to found what became a permanent institution. He sent her a considerable sum, authorising her to draw upon Murray and Sons at New York for $1000, "charging the same in the account of the world to come of my brother Philip and your brother Antonio. If something more should be wanted, you are commanded to quote it to me plainly and positively. Your prayers have so much bettered our mercantile importance here below, that in spite of all the embargoes, political and commercial troubles which have caused and will cause the utter ruin of many, we possess greater means now than before, thanks to God, with the same unalterable good-will." This secular school appears to have been carried on for about a year; and, although cherishing hopes for the future, when Mrs Seton began it she had no certain prospects of forming a society whose members would be especially consecrated to the service of

God. This deepening and enlargement came about little by little.

The first person who came to her with any such intention was a young lady, Miss Cecilia O'Conway, who was thinking of going to Europe and becoming a nun, but hearing of Mrs Seton's ultimate hopes she was induced to change her plan and remain in America. Her father accompanied her to Baltimore, and offered her to Mrs Seton as a child whom he consecrated to God, and on the 7th of December 1808 Miss O'Conway became her first companion and assistant in the school then under her charge; and the next person who started up was a student in St Mary's Seminary at Baltimore, a man of forty, who possessed fortune and had a great devotion for the children of the poor. He one day told M. Dubourg that if he could find someone to undertake a poor school he would give his money for that purpose, and he wondered if Mrs Seton would be willing to undertake it; so from one to another plans were taken up and developed. It was this middle-aged student, Mr Cooper, who chose the site of the now famous Emmettsburg, preferring the country to the city of Baltimore, and he seems to have made over a sum of $8000 (nearly £2000 of English money). M. Dubourg was thus enabled to buy the piece of land now held for so many years by the Sisters of Charity. The only tenement on the farm was a very small stone building, forming about one half of what was afterwards used as the wash-house of the institution, and it was settled in the joint tenantship of the Rev. William Dubourg, the Rev.

John Dubois, and the Rev. Samuel Cooper. And now occurred what always does occur in histories of religious foundations; people came in from the most unlikely quarters — people whom Mrs Seton had never heard of before. The second lady who offered herself as a candidate arrived from Philadelphia, and so did the third, and the fourth came from New York. Mrs Seton, who never thought much of herself, looked upon herself as unsuited to the task of forming a congregation for charitable work, as well as to the practice of life in religion, and at first shrank back with tears; but M. Dubourg said that the time had come for the four candidates to assume, as far as practicable, the form of a religious community. "She therefore proposed to the Sisters to appear in a habit like that which she wore herself, and which consisted of a black dress with a short cape, similar to a costume which she had observed among the religious of Italy. Her head-dress was a neat white muslin cap with a crimped border, and a black crape band around the head, fastened under the chin." She herself had worn this dress since the death of her husband. She asked that the little group should be called "Sisters of St Joseph," and this costume, to which they held for many years, was assumed on the 1st of June 1809. The next two candidates came from the city of Baltimore, Mrs Rose White, a widow lady, and Miss Catherine Mullen. The former became Superioress when Mrs Seton died. From year to year the new community went on increasing in numbers and in good works; but death struck grievous blows on the tender heart of the mother who had now become Mother Seton to so many spiritual daughters. That scourge of youth in the beginning of the century, consumption, struck two of her husband's sisters, who had successively joined her; but far more bitter were the deaths of two of her own daughters, the youngest and the eldest; for the beloved Anna, the favourite little daughter who had warmed herself with the skipping-rope in the cold quarantine at Leghorn, who had waited on her dying father, and knelt obediently and tenderly by his cold remains, was early called away. These children had undoubtedly inherited consumption, and what the mother's feelings were in witnessing the sufferings and rapid decline of each precious child can be better imagined than described. "With all the tenderness that maternal love could inspire, she watched day and night by the couch of her dying Anna, bestowing every care, and administering every comfort with the most unremitting attention, and being quite resigned to the will of God."

The last nine years of Mrs Seton's life witnessed the full expansion of the work which she had undertaken. As the story of one year must naturally resemble another in the methods pursued, we will only indicate the principal events that occurred in the years 1812 and 1813. The community received the regular services of the Rev. Simon Gabriel Bruté, who had been appointed the assistant of Father Dubois. He was one of the numerous French priests whose family fortunes had been scattered by the Revolution, even if they themselves had not been personally exiled. In 1813 eighteen members of Mrs Seton's community were fully professed, so that she was soon enabled to send workers to other places. The first fresh start was made in Philadelphia, where, for some years past, an asylum had been established for the adoption of children whose parents had fallen victims to the yellow fever. The trustees of Trinity Church were the managers of this asylum, and, with a view to its better organisation, they applied in 1814 for the services of the Sisters of Charity. It is not very clear whether the foundation had been originally Roman Catholic. Mother Seton was overcome with joy and gratitude at the opportunity of serving the poor orphans, and sent three Sisters, one of whom was the widow lady, Mrs Rose White. They travelled by land, as it was now September 1814, when Chesapeake Bay was infested with the hostile fleet of the British, and packet navigation was unsafe. For the purpose of saving expense, they were directed, as far as circumstances would permit, to ask help on the way, and they experienced much kindness from the Roman Catholic families who entertained them. It is needless to say that they flourished in their work, in spite of extreme poverty in the beginning. For three months they had no bread, save at their principal meal, but used potatoes much during the first year; in fact, potatoes were their chief sustenance. One day, the Sisters being too much occupied at home, an orphan was despatched to the market with $12\frac{1}{2}$ cents, all the money in the house, to buy a shin of beef. A few hours afterwards the child returned to the asylum with a large piece of meat, her 12½ cents, and 50 cents besides, telling the Sisters that an old market woman, finding she was one of the orphans, had given her the money and meat, and authorised them to call upon her for assistance whenever they were in want. The old woman became a generous friend of the institution. By the benevolence of herself and others, it gradually acquired ampler resources, and was enabled to maintain under its charitable roof an increasing number of orphans. It became in time a magnificent work. About the same time a small community, founded in Kentucky by a priest, entered into negotiations with Mrs Seton for a junction; but the negotiations failed, and they went on side by side. Somewhat later, the Right Rev. Dr Conolly, Bishop of New York, also applied to Mother Seton. It was her native place, and the selection of the Sisters who would be sent thither was a matter of no small importance. Her family, as already recorded, had been intensely opposed to her conversion, which had been followed by that of two of her husband's sisters, and she knew that any work undertaken in New York would be narrowly watched by her former acquaintance, and would reflect honour or discredit upon her profession, according to its result. She therefore moved Mother Rose White away from Philadelphia, and sent her to New York with Cecilia O'Conway and Felicité Brady. They set out on the 20th of June 1817. This new foundation also achieved an ample success; but the life of the ardent, energetic woman was fast drawing to its premature close. In 1818 she caught a violent inflammation of the lungs, from which she was with difficulty restored. She had been sorely tried by the death of her youngest daughter, Rebecca, who had also succumbed to the fatal malady inherent in William Seton's blood; and Mother Seton was now left with only one daughter and her two sons. She had sent the eldest, William, to her dear friends at Leghorn, and in writing to him about his young sister's death, she rises to a height quite extraordinary, for thus she tells him: "It would be selfish of us to have wished her inexpressible sufferings prolonged, and her secured peace deferred for our longer possession of this dear creature. Though in her I have lost the little friend of my heart, who read every pain or joy of it, and soothed by the most doting affection every daily care, the darling of my soul, through her so unexampled sufferings and patience, yet I look up with joy, and feel only for you, so far away. She said often, if it was possible to show herself to you, she would; but of one thing she was sure, our Lord would not refuse to let *her* see *you*, and from the heavenly grace He favoured her with in this world, we may well think He would refuse her nothing." This cherished son, William, had from the first a passion for the Navy, and he finally left Leghorn, his place being taken in the mercantile house by his younger brother. Philip Filiechi, the elder member of the firm, died before Mother Seton. He had been the best and most faithful of friends, and he was greatly mourned at Leghorn. Mrs

Seton never entirely recovered her severe illness of 1818, and two years later her health began seriously to fail. Her sailor son was then absent on a cruise; her second boy arrived from Italy during his mother's illness, but the situation of his affairs hurried him away, and he was not with her at the last. One only daughter remained by her side, and was by her on her deathbed, "sobbing bitterly." Of her there is nothing to record, as she was evidently living when the Life of Mrs Seton came to be written. At Mother Seton's deathbed she asked one of her attendants to recite her favourite prayer, "Soul of Christ, sanctify me, Body of Christ, save me, Blood of Christ, inebriate me, Water, out of the Side of Christ, strengthen me," but the Sister, overpowered by her grief, not being able to proceed, Mother Seton continued the prayer herself. Her last words were the sacred names of "Jesus, Mary, Joseph." "After this she lost the power of speech, and it appeared to the Sister who was next to her that the Lord was in a special manner at her side." She passed away at two o'clock in the morning, on the 4th of January 1821, in the forty-seventh year of her age.

Her place in the community was filled by Sister Rose White, whose age and experience best fitted her for the position. The Sisterhood then numbered fifty members, of whom forty were at that time at the Mother House. During Mother Rose's administration, colonies settled in Baltimore and in Washington, and at the towns of Lancaster and Frederick. The home school then counted about seventy pupils. In addition to these works, the Sisters took charge of the infirmary connected with the medical department of the University of Maryland. In the fifteen years following Mother Seton's death, free schools for the poor were opened at numerous towns; and when cholera fell heavily upon America, thirteen Sisters left for Philadelphia, and another set went into the city of Baltimore. Several of these Sisters were carried off by the pestilence. Mother Rose White survived until July 1841. It is impossible to detail the succession of foundations which were made up to the year 1850. In that year a very important step was taken, after frequent applications, for effecting a union between the Sisters of Charity in France and those in the United States. The request of the latter was at last granted, and the American Sisters were incorporated in the order founded by St Vincent of Paul. Thus they became members of that great band, numbered by thousands, and known all over the world, and they wear the white cornette.

On the wall of a humble chamber at Emmettsburg is an inscription which says: "Here by this fireplace, on a poor little couch died our cherished and sainted Mother Seton, on the 4th of January 1821. She died in poverty, but rich in faith and good works. May we, her children, walk in her footsteps and share one day in her blessings."

WILLIAM SETON, HUSBAND OF E. A. BAYLEY.

Appleton's "Cyclopædia of American Biography" says (vol. v. p. 465) that Mr Seton's father (1746-1798), who was also named William, "belonged to an impoverished noble Scottish family, emigrated to New York in 1758, and became superintendent and part owner of the iron-works of Ringwood, N.J. He was a loyalist, and the last royal public notary for the city and province of New York during the war. His silver notarial seal, dated 1779, is still in the possession of his family. He was ruined financially at the close of the Revolution, but remained in New York, where he founded the once famous mercantile house of Seton, Maitland & Co."

Mother Seton's grandson, William, an author, is stated in the same book to be "recognised by Burke's 'Peerage' as the head of the ancient family of the Setons of Parbroath, senior cadets of the Earls of Winton in Scotland."

AN AMERICAN POSTSCRIPT

THE story of the Californian mission of the Sisters of Mercy is so strangely unlike that of their other foundations that it is worthy of special record here. It began, as usual, with the demand of a bishop, Monsignor Alemany of San Francisco, who wanted a small colony for the distant mission of California. Dr Delaney, who was Bishop of Cork in the year 1854, was well acquainted with his episcopal brother on the "Sunset Slope"; and, after various pros and cons, it was settled that he should obtain what he wanted from the convent in Kinsale. Bishop Alemany had desired his ambassador, Father Gallagher, to obtain the nuns direct from Ireland, and indeed from Baggot Street; but Baggot Street had sent out so many colonies that it was just then poor in nuns, and sent him on to the large and flourishing community of Kinsale. California then being considered, as it truly was, an awful place, the Sisters were told that none but volunteers would be accepted. Those who were willing to go were told to write their names and put the papers in a box in the chapel. Nearly everybody volunteered, but Bishop Delaney allowed only five to go. The Superioress then selected Sister Baptiste Russell, who had but just left the novitiate; Sister de Sales Reddan, who was old enough to be her grandmother; Sister M. Bernard Dwyer, Sister M. Frances Benson, and Sister Mary Howley; and to these were added three novices who had the courage to offer themselves. The Superioress accompanied them to Dublin; and at Cork they were joined by five Presentation nuns who had accepted the Sacramento mission, for Father Gallagher had found it impossible to get a second body of Sisters of Mercy. They proposed to sail in the steamer *Arctic*, eighteen in number; but room failed, and not wishing to separate they deferred their departure till the starting of another boat called the *Canada*. The well-known convert, Dr Ives, had his baggage actually on board the *Arctic*, but, to have the pleasure of Father Gallagher's company during the voyage, he went to the trouble of removing it, and deferred his departure a week. Had he not done so, he and his wife would have perished with the rest on that ill-fated vessel. The *Canada* reached New York on the first Friday in October, and the nuns were received in a Convent of Mercy, formerly established in the city. Father Gallagher was obliged to go to Pennsylvania to conclude some business of great moment, and as the Sisters of Mercy were afraid to undertake their long and perilous journey without him, they remained in a New York convent for five weeks, when they started for the Isthmus of Panama. Going towards the Pacific was novel and interesting in the extreme, and though nothing occurred on their coasting journey along the States, they had plenty of experiences in Mexico. The heat was intense; sometimes they were on river boats, and sometimes they had to walk a considerable distance, for the arrangements seems to have become quite disorganised, and it is noted that they got hardly any sleep for four nights. When they got to Nicaragua they found a pretty little steamer awaiting them on the lake, which is about ninety miles long by forty broad; it is studded by islands of volcanic origin, and two or three were active when the Sisters passed them. The first sight of the Pacific gave them great delight; the Sisters gazed on it in silence from the beautiful shelving beach, and thanked God that they had reached the Ocean on whose shores they were to spend whatever remained of life. There was nothing like a wharf, and the steamer which was to take them up to Francisco stood far out in deep water. Father Gallagher presently appeared with four natives, whom he had induced to dress in linen shirts and pantaloons, and by them the Sisters were carried to the skiffs and rowed to the steamer, which they reached in time for supper. On this vessel was a motley assemblage of human beings—"wild creatures from every part of the earth, going in search of gold." The sea was calm, and the air balmy, and the Sisters got up very early in the morning, and had their morning prayers, office, and meditations finished before anybody came out of the state-rooms. They appear to have been several days on the voyage, and did not reach San Francisco Bay until midnight on the 7th December, and remained on board till five the next morning, actually landing on the Feast of the Immaculate Conception. They drove straight to St Patrick's Church, and reached it just as the old priest was turning to salute the congregation before the last gospel. The Sisters of Mercy were hospitably received by the Sisters of Charity, whose house joined St Patrick's Church. The archbishop and the vicar-general came later in the day to welcome them. Here they seem to have remained for nearly a month, and then got into a small, neat house of their own, containing six rooms and a kitchen, selected as being close to the county hospital. Their first visitation of the sick was made on the 4th January 1855. The Sisters were called in to see a dead woman, as it was supposed, for the poor creature had been found in that condition; they noticed signs of life. Immediately they sent for a priest, meanwhile employing the usual means of restoring animation. The poor woman revived, and was carried to the county hospital, where she lingered several months. They soon rented a house next door to their own, and in the beginning it was filled with children sent to San Francisco to await news of parents in the distant mining camps. It was often a long time before it was possible to notify the arrival of the little ones. Steamers then came once a month, and later twice a month. One fails to imagine the chances awaiting children thus tumbled out on to the shore of the Western State. After a time came cholera, and there the Sisters played their usual part; and, when that pestilence moderated, the Sisters were officially asked to assume the charge of the indigent school of the county of San Francisco, which they gladly did. This appointment was the cause of extreme rage on the part of one of the newspapers named the *Bulletin*. One of the physicians wrote an article

AN AMERICAN POSTSCRIPT

in defence, which concludes: "We cannot dismiss this subject without congratulating the public that we possess three departments that reflect credit upon us—the fire department, the schools, and the hospitals under the management of the Sisters of Mercy." The general state of the town appears to have been wild in the extreme. In 1856, James King, the editor of the *Bulletin*, was shot in the street by a gentleman whom he had slanderously attacked in his newspaper. He died, and a Vigilance Committee was formed, which seems to have partaken of the nature of a committee for Lynch law. Mr Casey, who shot Mr King, did not consider himself an assassin; rightly or wrongly, he thought his terrible provocation justified the act; but the Vigilance Committee held a secret session, in which they condemned him to death. He was desirous of being consoled by the Sisters of Mercy in the last days of his life, and Archbishop Alemany earnestly begged that favour for him. The Vigilants, however, refused the ministrations of the Sisters, but allowed him to have a priest. He died saying, "O Lord! have mercy on my enemies." His monument is in the church of Dolores, and that sentence is inscribed upon it under his name. Another singular person with whom the Sisters became closely connected was one Amanda Taylor, a Protestant woman, about thirty years of age, and a native of New Orleans. She had led a very bad life; and in August 1856, in what seems to have been a fit of nervous horror, she came to the Sisters and implored them to keep her, even in the coal-hole. Amanda was the kind of person with whom this little colony of Sisters had naturally no practical concern; their work did not lie that way, but they could not bear to send her off. They gave her a room, and every evening one of them took her for a little walk. She was not a pleasant person to deal with, being accustomed to a life of endless self-indulgence. In the beginning she would let the Sisters make her bed, sweep her room, and render her every menial service, while she rocked listlessly in a chair. But before a year had elapsed Amanda was an altered being. The Sisters picked up a very young girl, and gave her to Amanda to take care of; this proved a real God-send, and effected a great spiritual change.

One other story of the same kind may be quoted. A certain Chilian lady of the upper class, who seemed to have become almost idiotic, was abandoned by her evil associates, and fell into the hands of the nuns. When spoken to on ordinary matters she appeared to be deaf, never giving the slightest heed; but if religion were named or hinted at, she became furious. The Sisters were at their wits' end, and spoke to the archbishop. He called to see her, and was greeted by a torrent of the most awful language. "This," said he, "is not insanity; she is possessed by demons. You must do as our Lord prescribed, you must fast and pray," adding, in the words of Scripture, "This kind cometh not out except by prayer and fasting." He then suggested that the nuns should undertake a penitential fast with prayer. They divided themselves into nine bands, and each division took one day. When the ninth day was ended,

AN AMERICAN POSTSCRIPT

the Sister who was down first in the morning found Annetta standing at the hall door, dressed in the Spanish style for church, the folds of the heavy black silk lace mantilla covering her completely. They sent a trusty messenger to follow her discreetly through the streets. She went straight to the cathedral, and entered the archbishop's confessional, which he daily occupied very early in the morning. From that day till her death, three years afterwards, there was no more fury or bad language.

The Sisters during these first years underwent sufferings which they consider unfit to be put upon paper. They had to do with murderers, drunkards, Mormons, Indians, and Chinese. On Good Friday, 1856, as a party of them were turning the corner of a crowded street, they perceived the body of a man dangling on a rope stretched from house to house. Stunned and horrified, they began praying fervently for the poor wretch, whoever he might be. But the corpse was only an effigy of Judas, and, according to a Mexican custom, was hanged every Good Friday. It might have been worse, but is surely typical of the state of the public nerves. This and similar usages have long since been discontinued. Another terror was that of rats; a young priest going on a dark morning to the hospital was set upon by a troop of these little beasts, and ever after went in fear of his life.

A most pathetic story is that of a little Chinese girl, transported from the ship to the hospital; she threw herself into the arms of an Irish woman who stood by, saying: "The Chinese are bad, bad, bad." She had been stolen from her parents, who were evidently of the upper class. Once when she was ill a Chinese missionary was brought to her bedside, but nothing would induce her to listen to him; she could not believe he was a priest; she said, "No, no! Chinese man no priest; Chinese man bad man," and the Sisters were obliged to send for an old Irish Father. This little girl was baptised under the name of "Nora"; she died in 1860, being then about eighteen.

The most unmanageable patient ever received was "General Williams": his oaths and imprecations were fearful. "My dear," said the attending Sister to him one day, "you had better desist, for you may be in God's presence before morning." "Let me alone," he answered; "I do not care if I die like a dog." Him also they got round, and he died a peaceful and religious death.

One other case was that of "Tipperary Bill," who was really an American, named Martin; he had been for years a terrible outlaw, defying ruling power, and even "that travesty of justice, the Vigilance Committee." He was taken and chained, hands and feet, to an iron ring in a dark cell, and looked more like a savage than like a being of any degree of civilisation. His jailers were even then so much afraid of him that no one would approach him alone; but the Sisters found means to tame him, and prevented him from committing suicide. "Oh," he said, "if you knew how I had been tempted to self-destruction, you would feel how merciful to me has been the God to whom I go this morning."

AN AMERICAN POSTSCRIPT

It is now forty-four years since this little band of women from Kinsale landed in San Francisco; everything is altered now. The photograph of their beautiful hospital shows that it would do credit to London or Paris; they have asylums, schools, and convents all over the State, and there is at least one noted survivor of the first band, a woman full of years and honour, who has lived to see the great change in the "Golden West."

The particulars of the Californian Mission were obtained with some difficulty from a volume of the Annals after the completion of the rest of this book. It will be remarked that the Sisters of Mercy were received by the Sisters of Charity, who were already established in San Francisco.

W. H. WHITE AND CO. LTD.
RIVERSIDE PRESS, EDINBURGH

Messrs Duckworth & Co.'s
New Books

THE SAINTS

THE series is under the general editorship of M. HENRI JOLY, formerly Professor at the Sorbonne and at the Collège de France, author of numerous works upon Psychology; and the authorised English translations are having, and will continue to have, the advantage of the revision of the Rev. Father TYRRELL, S.J., who contributes to each volume a Preface and, in some cases, a few Notes addressed especially to English readers.

In order to give a true idea of the nature of the volumes, the publishers give below some passages from the letter addressed by the General Editor of the series to his collaborators.

"In a very remarkable letter upon the true method of writing the lives of the Saints, Mgr. Dupanloup did not hesitate to say that, 'there are very few lives of the Saints written as they should be,' and he asks for this work, 'Above and beyond everything else a love of the Saint, then a profound study of his life and spirit from original sources and contemporary documents, then the portraiture of this soul and its struggles, and of what nature and grace were in it; all this traced with simplicity, truthfulness, dignity, deep penetration, and impressive detail, in such a way that the Saint and his times may be faithfully represented, but nevertheless so that the presentation of the contemporary facts of history may not blur the picture of the Saint, who should always remain the most prominent figure in his story; true and authentic facts, briefly set forth, but arranged with skill and cleverly disposed, in a scholarly sequence, preparing for and illuminating everything;' — the precaution of 'making the Saint himself tell his own story, without which everything living and individual is apt to disappear, and thus all Saints are made to resemble one another . . . a style, in short, simple, reverent, touching, and penetrative.'

"That all these qualities have been often enough united in works worthy of being studied we are very far from denying . . . but it has been in the case of quarto books or in works in more than one volume. It has, therefore, been thought opportune to present a living portrait of each of the great Saints in a more restrained form, in order to draw attention to it, and perhaps to re-form the ideas of a much larger circle of readers."

The following passage, taken from an article by the English editor in *The Month* for December 1897, entitled "What is Mysticism?" will also be of use as a further indication of the spirit in which the books are being written:—

"The old time-honoured Saint's Life, with its emphasis on the miraculous and startling features of the portrait, its suppression of what was natural, ordinary, and, therefore, presumably uninteresting, and consequently its abandonment of all attempt to weave the human and divine into one truthful and harmonious whole, showing the gradual evolution of the perfect from the imperfect, to many minds makes no appeal whatever . . . All this points to the need of what we might call a more subjective treatment of Saints' lives than we have been accustomed to; and it is to this that the 'Psychologie des Saints' addresses itself. We need less than formerly to be dazzled with the wonderful, and more to be drawn to the lovable. We want to be put *en rapport* with the Saints, to feel their humanity, to interpret it by our own, and thereby to realise that no miracle they ever wrought is comparable to the miracle of what they were."

The first volumes are as follows:—

THE PSYCHOLOGY OF THE SAINTS

By HENRI JOLY, formerly Professor at the Sorbonne and at the Collège de France. Author of "L'homme et l'animal"; "Psychologie des grands hommes," etc.

Weekly Register (leading article).—"To humanise the Saints in a wider and broader way, founded on a more comprehensive survey of human powers, is the task which has been essayed by M. Joly. This object is brought out by Fr. Tyrrell, S.J., in an admirable preface, possessing the literary touch to a degree not over-common in modern religious writings."

Academy.—"A very ably-written little book. A clever and valuable attempt to apply modern methods to ancient problems. M. Joly comes to his difficult task unusually well-equipped. He is helped by science; he is helped, also, by his study of the psychology of genius. This latter is a peculiar advantage for his task, which he shares with no previous student of the subject that we can recollect."

Church Review.—"As a study of what is noblest, purest, and best in humanity it is bright, cheerful, and invigorating."

Catholic Herald.—"One of the most remarkable and valuable contributions to the literature of hagiology that has been published in recent years."

S. AUGUSTINE

By AD. HATZFELD, joint-collaborator with Arsène Darmesteter in the "Dictionnaire Général de la Langue Française." Translated by E. HOLT.

Outlook. — "The whole book may be unreservedly commended as an excellent and compendious account of Augustine's life and introduction to his works, stripped of controversial matter or needless personal comment."

The Month.—"The general result will be the familiarising of the ordinary educated public with the true personality of one who is to so many little more than a name."

S. CLOTILDA

By GODEFROY KURTH, Professor at the University of Liège. Author of "Histoire poetique des Mérovingiens," "Clovis," etc. Translated by V. M. CRAWFORD.

S. VINCENT DE PAUL

By PRINCE EMMANUEL DE BROGLIE, Lauréat de l'Académie française. Translated by MILDRED PARTRIDGE.

Further volumes will be announced in due course.

*Small Crown 8vo. Art vellum,
Gilt top, 3s. each volume.*

THE UNKNOWN SEA

A Romance. By CLEMENCE HOUSMAN. Crown 8vo, art vellum, dull gold top. 6s.

Literature.—"The idea is a strange and poetic one, and the book has an atmosphere. On the conception of Christian the author may be congratulated. He is ideal without sentimentality, and his sacrifice and death have the poignancy of reality, symbol though he is of the world's greatest idea. The reader must pocket his criticising spirit and simply give himself up to the spell of the writer of 'The Unknown Sea.' He has imagination, charm, and a haunting Celtic sadness about his style, that one does not often meet with."

Guardian.—"Decidedly powerful and effective. Its author has certainly a spell by which, like the Ancient Mariner, he can force people to listen to and accept his tale."

St James's Gazette.—"The qualities that commend this book are its fitting impression of the supernatural, its studied and generally successful use of words, and its appreciation of the beauty of visible things. It achieves an absolute effect of beauty; an effect of a kind that is extremely rare in English that is not verse. The book has beauty and sense—not, thank heaven, common-sense!—in it, and is quite remote from the common trash of the book market."

Pall Mall Gazette.—"The story is a powerful one, stirring the imagination with vague suggestions of mystery, and compelling interest throughout."

Nottingham Daily Guardian.—"The poetry and mysticism of the story are its great charms. A delicate fancy and a rich imagination have enabled the author to invest it with singular impressiveness. The reader need not be envied who can lay aside the book unfinished, nor, let it be added, who is unable to appreciate the dainty fashion in which the tale is treated. 'The Unknown Sea' is not a popular novel; there is too much really fine work in it for that, but hardly a page fails to indicate the author's delicate methods and robust individuality."

Newcastle Chronicle.—"'The Unknown Sea' is a novel, but it is like no other novel. It is the most exquisite allegory that has been written for a long time. In the unhappy and ascetic passion of Christian, the fisherman, for Diadyomene, the maiden of the sea, we may read obscurely the secular struggle of spirit and flesh. But the allegory may be what it will. The story is justified of itself, and has a certain palely imaginative quality that is of a strange delicacy."

Aberdeen Free Press.—"A writer of rare promise. The theme is original, and its treatment is marked by a degree of imaginative power that is weirdly impressive. One of the most remarkable stories that has been put in our hands for a considerable period."

THE FIRE OF LIFE

A Novel. By CHARLES KENNETT BURROW. Crown 8vo, cloth. 6s.

St. James's Gazette.—"A clever story. The smoothly-written little tale, with its rather ambitious title, is a real pleasure to read, because it has a wholesome, manly tone about it, and the characters do not appear to be book-made, but of real flesh and blood."

Outlook.—"It has a point of view, a delicate sensitiveness, artistic restraint, subtlety of perception, and a true literary style. Mr Burrow proves himself an artist with many sides to his perception."

Standard.—"Mr Burrow's book is well-written and amusing."

Saturday Review.—"A good, careful, full-blooded novel of a kind that is not common nowadays."

Literary World.—"Had we passed it by unread, ours would have been the loss. A charming story, based on somewhat conventional lines, but told with such verve and freshness as render it really welcome. Mr Burrow has admirably succeeded in writing a really interesting story, and, which is more uncommon, he has well individualised the different persons of his drama. 'The Fire of Life' should figure in the list of novels to be read of all those who like a good story, and like that good story well told."

Yorkshire Post.—"A book of rare strength and charm. With a simple plot Mr Burrow moves us profoundly—one of the good tests of a true craftsman. 'The Fire of Life' is a book of the season."

Manchester Courier.—"This is one of those delightful domestic stories that are always welcome. The book is full of vigorous character. The whole book is full of 'fire,' full of 'life,' and full of interest."

Nottingham Express.—"It is one of those novels which one does not care to leave off once it has been started, and its brevity and fascination make it quite possible to read it at a sitting without much inconvenience. The author's style is clear and crisp, with a purity of diction which it would be difficult to surpass."

Scotsman.—"Readable and enjoyable to a degree seldom reached by tales of the kind. It is always happy when it touches the external life in which it is set."

Dundee Advertiser.—"It is a sweet, wholesome tale. The music-master's portrait is admirably drawn, and remains in the memory. A lover of the country will linger over the delicious pictures of the olden village around which most of the scenes are set. The author is at his best in the delicate passages, where he secures some exquisite effects."

Glasgow Herald.—"The characters are more human and endowed with more individuality than the creations of many novelists."

Large Crown 8vo. Price 7s. 6d.

DR KARL WITTE'S ESSAYS ON DANTE
Translated by C. MABEL LAWRENCE, B.A. Edited by PHILIP H. WICKSTEED, M.A.

During the whole of the central portion of this century Dr Karl Witte was actively engaged in Dante studies, and his translations, editions, and essays constitute a more important contribution to the revived and deepened study of Dante than any other single scholar can boast to have made. He is the acknowledged master of Scartazzini, Giuliani, and others; and in especial, his conception of Dante's Trilogy (that is to say, his idea as to the mutual relations of the Vita Nuova, the Convito, and the Comedy) underlies all subsequent work on the inner meaning and articulation of Dante's writings. Dr Witte collected the essays in which this and many subsidiary points are elaborated in two volumes. They are published at the high price of £1, 8s., which makes them out of the reach of many, even of those Dante students to whom the languages in which they are written (German for the most part, but occasionally Italian) offer no difficulties. Some of them are of little interest to the general circle of Dante students, dealing as they do with German translations of the Comedy or German works on Dante; but the remaining essays constitute an invaluable body of investigations, of great variety of interest, ranging from a general survey of Dante's mental development or a presentation of his conception of the universe, to the discussion of biographical details or the identification of the authors and relative antiquities of ancient commentaries. The proposed translation will include all of Dr Witte's essays that have any general interest.

In an Introduction, and in special notes in the several essays, the editor will give the student the means of checking Dr Witte's results in doubtful or speculative matters by reference to the original sources, or to essays written from another point of view, but he will carefully abstain from fretting the reader by a running commentary of criticism interrupting the essays themselves.

www.ingramcontent.com/pod-product-compliance
Lightning Source LLC
Chambersburg PA
CBHW021817230426
43669CB00008B/777